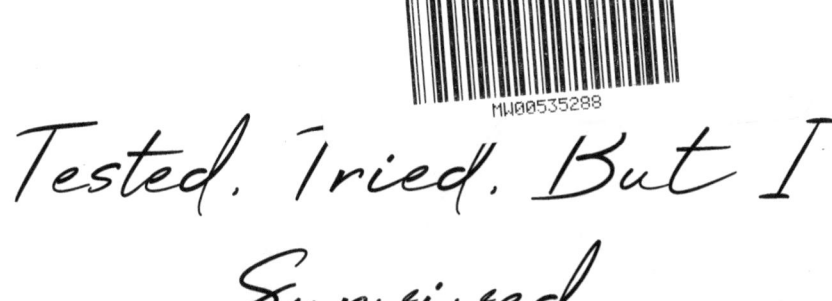

Tested, Tried, But I Survived

Kimberly Moses & Co-authors

REJOICE
Essential Publishing

Tested, Tried, But I Survived/Kimberly Moses & Co-authors

ISBN-13: 978-1-956775-29-7

Introduction

By Kimberly Moses

We will all go through trials in life, but you will overcome them if you have faith in God. Some are dealing with a loss of a loved one, economic pressure, divorce, relationship drama, rebellious children, toxic work environment, sickness in their body, mental attacks, stress, financial problems, and more. If we aren't careful, worrying can cause us to die prematurely. God promises us long life and it isn't His will for us to leave this earth before our appointed time. Yet many do because they don't have faith in God, lack wisdom, or are disobedient. There are many different seasons we experience in life *(Matthew 5:45)*. Sometimes when it rains, it pours. When it rains, it rains on the just and the unjust. Being a good person has nothing to do with the things you will experience through life. David was a good person and a man after God's heart *(1 Samuel 13:14)*. Still, he experienced being rejected by his father *(1 Samuel 16:10-11)*, his son raped his daughter *(2 Samuel 13)*, his son trying to steal his kingdom *(2 Samuel 15)*, his leader trying to kill him multiple times *(1 Samuel 19)*. Yet he still trusted God to deliver. Joseph

1

was a good person, but his brothers hated him *(Genesis 37:4)*. His brothers sold him into slavery *(Genesis 37:12-36)*. His master's wife tried to sleep with him and lied on him. He was imprisoned for a crime he didn't commit *(Genesis 39)*. However, these two men are examples of surviving the trials. What should have broken them didn't because they had God on their side.

Initially, many don't believe in God's miraculous power to deliver until they get in a situation and call unto Him. Amazingly, God answers. For instance, have you ever prayed something along the lines of, *"God, if you get me out of this, I will serve you."* As a result, God answered your prayer, but it was up to you to honor the vow you made unto Him. With God, you can survive each trial because He is with you. When there was a storm, Jesus was with the disciples. The storm raged so much that it rocked the ship violently and the disciples were afraid. However, Jesus managed to sleep through it because He knew that everything was going to be okay. The disciples woke up Jesus and Jesus spoke to the storm and miraculously, it obeyed and there was now a great peace *(Mark 4:35-41)*. As we go through trials in life, we must trust in Jesus because He will speak to our storms by causing a great stillness. We can find comfort knowing that the storms will come in our lives, but they won't kill us because we have Jesus on our side.

"Tested, Tried, But I Survive" is about God's miraculous hand. We must learn how to see God in the storm. God promises to illuminate our darkness or shine His glory upon our gloomy situations *(Psalm 18:28)*. This is a collaboration of testimonies of real accounts. Each testimony is about a survivor of various trials. God is no respecter of a person *(Acts 10:34)*. If He rescued the people in this book, He will do it for you. Know that you are next in line for your miracle.

As you read each chapter, you will gather wisdom on navigating your challenges. Allow this manuscript to mentor you in your purpose and assignment. We will discuss the following topics to empower you for your journey ahead:

- Finances
- Sickness
- Marriage
- Children
- Witchcraft
- Nursing school
- Homelessness
- Abandonment
- Foster care
- Juvenile justice
- Grief
- Deadly accidents
- The consequences of disobedience
- Covid-19.

Pay careful attention to how God brought each person out and the wisdom they acquired so you can learn from their challenges. Before continuing in this book, take a moment to pray to make Jesus your Lord and Savior if He isn't already. Tomorrow isn't promised to anyone and life is but a vapor *(James 4:14)*. If you were to die tonight, you need to know if you would make it into heaven. It's not by circumstance that you are reading this book.

Dear Lord,

I realized that I wouldn't make it into heaven and spend eternity with you if I were to die right now. I don't want to spend eternity in hell and being separated from your presence. I believe that you died on the cross for my sins. I confess that you rose from the dead on the 3rd day (Romans 10:9). I believe that your blood that was shed on Calvary washes away my sins. I yield myself to you. Come into my heart now. I make you Lord of my life in Jesus' name. Amen.

If you prayed that prayer, know that the angels in heaven are rejoicing *(Luke 15:10)*. Jesus leaves the other 99 sheep and goes after that 1 *(Matthew 18:12)*. You were the one today. You are special to God. Please don't ever make the mistake of running away from God because of trials. Run to God for comfort, peace, joy, hope, and strength during these difficult times. God never promised us that we wouldn't go through anything. However, He promises He will never leave us nor forsake us *(Deuteronomy 31:6)*. Welcome to the Body of Christ. Find a ministry where they teach the truth of the Gospel of Jesus Christ, read your Bible daily, and start developing a prayer and fasting lifestyle. Don't forget to get baptized or submerged in water which symbolizes the burial of your sins, to walk in new beginnings as you are now a new creature in Christ *(2 Corinthians 5:17)*. Lastly, seek the Lord for the infilling of the Holy Spirit with the evidence of speaking in other tongues. You need the Holy Spirit to fight this good fight of faith successfully. Now let's continue and find out how to survive being tested and tried.

CHAPTER 1

Abandonment

By Sandi S. Pizarro

According to Oxford Languages, the definition of abandonment is the action or fact of abandoning or being abandoned. WebMD[1] states abandonment issues stem from a fear of loneliness, which can be a phobia or a form of anxiety. These issues can affect your relationships and often stem from a childhood loss. Early childhood experiences are the biggest contributors to developing abandonment issues when you become an adult. The traumatic events might include the loss of a parent by divorce or death or not getting enough physical or emotional care as a child. Emotional abandonment occurs when parents do the following:

*Do not let their children express themselves emotionally,

* Ridicule their children

1. Contributors, WebMD Editorial. "Abandonment Issues: 3 Types of Attachment Styles." WebMD. WebMD. Accessed June 4, 2022. https://www.webmd.com/mental-health/abandonment-issues-symptoms-signs.

* Putting too much pressure on their children to be "perfect"
* Treat their children as their peers.

Abandonment issues happen when a parent or caregiver does not provide the child with consistent warm or attentive interactions, leaving them feeling chronic stress and fear. The experiences during a child's development will often continue into adulthood. This is why abandonment issues become more prevalent as you get older and affect your relationships.

Common signs of abandonment issues in adults include:
- Giving too much or being overly eager to please.
- Jealousy in your relationship or of others.
- Trouble trusting your partner's intentions.
- Feeling insecure about your relationship.
- Having difficulty in feeling intimate emotionally.
- Needing to control or be controlled by your partner.

I SURVIVED

The year was 2003, and I was in a season of my life where things were going well, or so I thought. My husband and I had been married only five months before we moved into a new apartment, giving us much more space to accommodate our newly expanded family. Then the unthinkable happened. One afternoon my husband left to shoot hoops with his friends as he often did, but what made this time so different was that evening, he never returned home. Of course, my mind started thinking the worse since he didn't call to inform me that he had other plans after playing basketball. On numerous occasions, I checked over at his friend's home in order to discover his whereabouts. I remember them telling me that they had not seen or heard from him nor knew where he could be. I later found out that they lied. I even called to check with my mother-in-law, who lived over a thousand miles away. The communication barrier was a hot mess. When trying to ask if she knew where he was, she spoke no English at the time. That is when I realized that I had to attempt to move on with my everyday life while believing that God was in control of the matter. I would periodically receive phone calls from him being coerced into telling me that he'd started a new life, he wasn't coming back home, the divorce papers were in the mail, and I shouldn't hesitate to sign them once I was presented with them. Even though I could discern that something wasn't right each time he called to say these things, it was still a major challenge for me to keep the faith in knowing that God was in control of my life and the things happening daily. I can say that's one of the first times I can remember facing spiritual warfare since I had given my life to Christ. Now that I think about it, I hadn't been taught about warfare and had no idea what I was dealing with nor how to handle it.

After some time had passed, I was still working part-time, getting paid nowhere near enough to pay all the bills by myself. I would go to food pantries weekly to provide dinner and to churches and other participating organizations to get funding to pay the important bills. All the luxuries had to cease, which meant no cable, internet, or other unnecessary things. In the midst of it all, God showed me favor with the property manager when I had to muster up enough courage to go and explain my situation and why I could no longer afford to live there. He first suggested that I downgrade to a one-bedroom that cost less to give me the ability to complete the duration of the lease. The next day the owner called me to meet with him again. I panicked because the enemy kept whispering that the man had changed his mind and was going to ask me to leave the premises at once. When I went to see him, to my surprise, he extended mercy. He allowed me to stay in the three-bedroom apartment and pay the amount of the one bedroom since it would probably be too pricey for me to rent a moving truck. God continued to show Himself throughout this ordeal. Once it was time to move, my pride wouldn't let me reach out to my family for help, so I lived in my car for a short period because of a lack of money for another apartment. I didn't want anyone to find out that my husband had left me. My daughter and I eventually went to a shelter after two weeks of sleeping on the balcony of "THD" 24-hour place of prayer, which was formally the church house that we attended for Sunday service.

My relationship with God had been restored through lack and nothing taking precedence in my life other than Him. What the devil meant for my downfall and destruction, God turned it into strength and a closer walk with Him. When I would stay overnight in the prayer center, I would often walk through the pews at 1 or 2 AM after getting off work. I prayed, read my Bible, and listened for revelation.

One night while in devotion, God revealed to me that even though He didn't cause the separation *(Matthew 12:25, KJV)*, He allowed it to take place so that I could give Him my undivided attention as I did three years prior, when I first received salvation. Before I married, I was totally sold out to God. I would participate in overnight shut-ins' every Friday and would not allow any secular music or TV shows in my home. I also fasted twice a week and prayed daily for three years straight. God was my everything. He also brought to my remembrance that I did not inquire of Him about the date that my husband and I were to marry. I used the scripture *1 Corinthians 7:9* (KJV) *...For it is better to marry than to burn,"* to win my argument for not asking Him about His plans for my marriage date, but in the end, God will always win. My husband and I are back together. We are going on nineteen years of marriage. We made a vow to each other to make this our first and last marriage, so no matter what happens, we'll tough it out by God's grace and mercy. With God first, this threefold cord is unstoppable.

<u>TAKE AWAY LESSON:</u>

- God is a jealous God; He will be first in your life one way or another. Don't put anything or anyone before your relationship with the Lord God Jehovah!! — *Exodus 34:14*

- Always have a nest egg saved up for a rainy day because an unexpected disaster can take place in your life at any moment.

- Always strengthen your prayer life more and more to sustain the winter seasons when they come. They will come, no matter how good things may be going *(1st Thessalonians 5:17)*. Prayer will also make it easier for you when you must completely trust in God to work it out. Study the Word to have scripture to stand on and fight within the spirit.

- Put your pride on the back burner and ask for help to get back on your feet. I was willing to live in my car in the hot summer heat just to keep my family from finding out what I was going through because of pride. — *Proverbs 11:2 (KJV)*

- Red flags: pay attention to any little things that are said in a nonchalant way but brought to your attention on more than one occasion or to ongoing disagreements. My husband was an introvert and therefore, he really didn't express himself at the beginning of our marriage, but there were signs that I ignored. So, I suggest that you keep your eyes and ears open.

- Never burn your bridges. In other words, don't destroy friendships over small insignificant things because you can't see in the future and you don't know who God may have on assignment to assist you in a particular season.

- Be always cordial with everyone. I know it's easier said than done, but even the Bible reminds us that we shall reap what we sow *(Galatians 6:7)*. In hard times, a good rapport can make or break you.

CHAPTER 2

Death of A Child

By Arlene Housey

Children are a gift from God that brings joy and happiness. They are an incredibly special part of us that gives us love and joy. The loss of a child can be a devastating moment in someone's life. The loss can change your life to help someone go through their loss. I lost my child when she was six years old. It took a while to talk about her death which stayed bottled up inside me for years. I had to find a place to be comfortable with making my heart be at one with God. The fight for my child to live taught me to have patience and allow God to do a work in my life. The finances of taking care of a child with health issues can be costly. I realized that it could help someone heal but can never recover.

My daughter was diagnosed with hydrocephalus at birth. Hydrocephalus is a chronic condition that builds up fluid within the brain. The excess fluid applies pressure on the brain. The doctors gave her a life expectancy of six months to live. When news like this is given to you about your child or loved one, it can scare you into giving up on life. As a young woman, I had one chance to turn to God. I had only my faith. It was weak at the time. I had to dig deep inside of myself to find strength. The testing of my faith began when I asked God to let my child live. I had to repent for the remission of sins to start the renewal of my relationship with God. I began to see signs of God in her life. There were changes in new reports that were promising to extend her life.

My life began to change due to the changes in her life. I found refuge in *Psalm 27:1. "The Lord is my light and my salvation; whom shall, I fear? The Lord is the strength of life, of whom shall I be afraid?"* I made this scripture a vital part of my daily routine to read from the Bible. I would go to the doctor's appointments and they would be amazed that she was still alive. The prayers that I petitioned to God daily were the key to building my faith on this journey. I started fasting once per week and then adding more days to make it a routine to help me build strength. God began to work a miracle, for she continued to improve by gaining weight and laughing.

The doctor decided to perform surgery on her due to the hydrocephalus. The surgery was to reduce some pressure on her brain. The surgery was a success and gave me more things to give God thanks for life. I realized she was a fighter too. We do not know how much pain a child can go through when sickness is in their body. As I watched her go through a quick recovery process. She was back smiling with us and enjoying listening to music. At this time, she passed the six-month mark of her life expectancy. She began to beat the odds of growing. If anyone ever imagines beating the odds against your life, it is the work of God. God knows what is best for our lives. I met so many people that gave me so much support for her. The obstacles were still against me due to her health problems. I had to realize that people can be cruel. The whispers about your child, but people do not realize it could have been them. I began to take her to church. It played an integral part for us until a pastor did not want to pray for us. I felt like God left me in my spirit so broken that there was nothing to say to anyone in the church. I always heard people talk about church hurt. It led me to be careful about allowing people to pray for my daughter.

TRIED

As the years progressed, she approached her sixth birthday. She faced a major setback of having seizures which led to additional hospitalizations. Her body began to change with her age. I prayed so hard for God to allow her to walk and talk. The seizures made her stop interacting at times with everyone around her. Her brain began to increase in size and the seizures became more frequent at times. I would always spend several nights at the hospital to let her know I was there. I had a full-time job but still made it to work on four or five hours of sleep. I always had that extra energy to make it through the day. I know my faith was always on the line. As a mother, you never get tired but keep pushing through. We go through situations that may make us turn away from God. I had to stand on my words with God. If you stand on the Word of God, nothing can shake your faith. I was my child's only advocate. Knowing that someone did not want to pray for you made me realize that all people are not bad.

For one thing, it did not make me stop taking my child to church. I know my faith was tested like someone on trial. She was hospitalized during the Christmas holidays of 2000. The doctors tried another surgery to help relieve some of the pressure then they discovered brain cancer. She never made it back home. The doctors gave up on her due to the progression of the cancer in her brain. I experienced one of the hardest holidays ever. It crushed my world to pieces. I could not talk for a while. I could not question God, but I just did not let go of my prayers for her. I am a person who believes in the impossible. If God raised Jairus's daughter, He could do it for mine (*Matthew 9:18-26*). Her recovery began to deteriorate over the weeks in the hospital. We had to move her into hospice care due to the surgery. The cancer began to weaken her body. At that point, she was very fragile. She passed away five days after being admitted into hospice care. I did not stop praying, but I had allowed God to do His work for my daughter. I had to realize that God had her in a better place. I know to lose a child is a devastating situation to go through. To be absent from the body is to be present with the Lord (*2 Corinthians 5:7-9*).

SURVIVAL

You never get over losing a child but reflect on the memories to cherish. My family played a major part in helping me with my daughter. The rebuilding of my relationship with God was an integral part of increasing my faith. I realize that God wanted my daughter in a much better place. I did not talk much about her death for some time. I knew you must be careful of telling any and everyone your business. I had a visitation from my daughter in a dream shortly after her death. I never had an experience like this in my life. She wanted to tell me the good news about heaven. She told me that heaven is a beautiful place with milk and honey. The milk and honey taste so good. I was so amazed to hear her talk to me. I started to shed tears, knowing she was there and watching over me. The streets are so beautiful and paved with gold. There is always fresh manna to eat. It is good to eat. She visited a few more times with me to share more wonderful things about heaven. The visitation from her was so exciting because I heard the good news that she would tell me about heaven.

God would allow me to hear her play games with other children. The most beautiful visitation was when I saw her walk into my room one night.

The prayer that I rendered to God for her to walk came true. I will never forget how she thanked me for taking care of her. I had to realize Crystal belonged to God. He needed her to work for him. At that point, I needed to continue my faith in God. I always have memories to share with the people around me. I started to share my story with other people to inspire them. I realize God is still good to us if we allow Him to take control and do not worry.

What I have learned in this part of my life:
- Stand on the Word of God.
- Fast and pray more to build a solid foundation with God.
- Allow God to have His way in your life no matter what you are going through.
- A loss can be a situation to help someone.
- I learned from my loss: do not be angry with God.
- Walk upright in humility.
- Family is a blessing to have.
- God loves us dearly.
- Be patient.

CHAPTER 3

Extraordinary Family History & Entrepreneurship

Father God Is Rewriting My Story

By Keima S Sinclair

"But the God of all grace, who hath called us unto his eternal glory by Christ Jesus, after that ye have suffered a while, will himself restore you and make you strong, firm, and steadfast."— 1 Peter 5:10 KJV

I am blessed to share my family background and testify with my personal stories from a place of confusion, brokenness, foolery, deliverance, humbleness, healing, grace, and restoration.

My late grandparents D. George and Mable Esther B. Thomas had a background working the fields of cotton and managing their farm in the south. My grandmother received her full education. However, my grandfather had received limited education because he had to work in the fields from when he was in the 3rd grade. After years had gone by, they married and when they could afford to, they moved northeast. One of my grandfather's stories stayed near and dear to my heart which encourages me to this very day. When my grandfather couldn't find work, he became creative and dedicated himself to work even if the work he did couldn't pay him. He remained faithful. My grandfather went out looking for work every day and was told several times that they weren't hiring. He had the faith that one day, it would come to pass, and he will be able to work and provide for his family. My grandfather was drawn to this one store with apartments on top. He decided to ask if the owner was hiring and he answered, "He was not hiring." My grandfather was willing to work for little money and the store owner gave him a smart remark (being sarcastic). So, he was persistent and came to the store and cleaned and swept in front of the store every day for free. After showing up every day to clean up and sweep the grounds, the store owner told him to come inside the store and said, "You are hired."

Grandpa did not know how to read as he barely completed the 3rd grade. In spite of this, he had plans or dreams to become a homeowner and worked very hard for years to achieve that goal. They worked very hard and saved their earnings. They were blessed to purchase their first house in the north, which they have occupied and turned their dwelling into a rental property and rented rooms. My grandparents became entrepreneurs and Real Estate Investors. Then after some time, they became the owners of additional property and had also opened and owned the second black-owned restaurant in the Great City of Paterson in New Jersey called 'City Restaurant.' People from afar heard about and shared great things about their restaurant. My grandmother was the cook along with her sons and daughters. My grandmother also served her customers and did some cashiering too. Her oldest daughter was a seamstress and sewed the curtains to the restaurant's windows. Each one of her children had a role in the operation of their restaurant.

Their burgers and brownies were a customer's favorite. The white high school kids would come every day after school mainly to buy their freshly made brownies and the African American high school kids would come to buy other food on the menu and some of them put their money in the Jukebox to play music and dance or sing along.

My grandmother taught her children how to make fresh grape jelly from their grapevine. My grandmother's mother, Viola, was educated and an entrepreneur also. She was a landowner and sold property and goods she made from her own farm and land down south. She did her own bookkeeping of the things she did. I remember reading an old penmanship letter she wrote, and in that letter, she expressed negotiating the sale of her land and property to a potential buyer. She wore many hats and her entrepreneurship skills inspired me.

In the end, my grandparents had owned residential and commercial property (mixed-use), lots, and land, and they were able to leave an inheritance to their children. It is an honor to be their grandchild and I adored their relationship with the Lord Heavenly Father. I was blessed to witness their dedication in marriage, partnership, and hard work with integrity and their friendliness and compassion for others. My grandparents' enthusiasm for property ownership and business was one of a kind. Their journey wasn't easy, but it was worth it all. I am truly grateful and blessed by the humble lives they led and the foundation they laid out for the generations that will come after them. *Proverbs 13:22, "A good man leaves an inheritance to his children's children..."*

One of the desires of my grandfather was to be a white-collar. He worked as a blue-collar from barely a 3rd grader for most of his life. I want to thank my grandfather because the majority of my work is a white-collar and I really enjoy what I do. Sometimes the dreams or desires of one generation are fulfilled in the next generation(s). My grandparents left their mark in the world, and it is up to their children and grandchildren and our children and theirs to do the same and leave a legacy and help bring salvation to the world. The Lord God is our firm foundation.

Father God Is Rewriting My Story

"For God wanted them to know that the riches and glory of Christ are for you Gentiles, too. And this is the secret: Christ lives in you. This gives you assurance of sharing His glory. So, we tell others about Christ, warning everyone and teaching everyone with all the wisdom God has given us. We want to present them to God, perfect in their relationship to Christ." Colossians 1:27-28 NLT

I came from a family of faith with standards and boundaries with an ethical, hard-working background. One day I did something different and out of the ordinary. I decided to take my own path. I had jobs working for myself, styling hair on campus at school, working as a Cashier and Telemarketer. Whatever I did, it was done with my whole heart working in excellence to the best of my ability and sometimes I'll go beyond. I was recognized for my work and mannerism, etc., by customers who rewarded me with cash gifts. I would receive notice from the managers warning me that receiving money was against work policy.

One job that I really liked had moved out of state. So, then I had to look for another job. When it seemed that I could not find a new job, one advertisement stood out to me. It stated, No Experience and Good $$$$$ daily, etc. When I went for an interview, the position was for being a topless masseuse. I was hesitant at first, but I figured there was no other job opportunity available for me, so why not give it a chance. Besides, the other gals and guy there seemed to be happy. I took the job, but I was not 100% proud of myself because I knew I had to keep this job a secret from my loved ones. I had to have a stage name, so I used the name "Monique." I have enjoyed the tips to get things, pay bills and help others. But it was a very intense and lustful environment in which I worked.

On one evening, it happened to be slow, with not many clients coming through. One of the young ladies had left work early. So, my boss and I were working to finish up and close. That evening was one of the scariest times I had faced in my life. We had experienced our lives being threatened. After two of the men's massage sessions were over, one of the men pointed a gun to my head while I was on the phone with my fiancé. He seemed like he could not do anything for me but became a little frightened. He was really the only person who knew what I was doing. The man holding the gun advised me to get off the phone immediately. He asked for the money the business made plus our tips. After the initial shock, I thought I had better act and quickly made up a story. And so, I explained to them that our Security regularly comes to check on us and collect the money. He yelled, "Don't lie to me. I don't want to hear it! Give me the money!" Eventually, I turned to God to say a quiet prayer for help. They cursed us out badly and threatened to pull the trigger if we did not give them the money. Yet, we stood by our stories. They refused to leave without getting what they came for. The client holding the gun was sweating and seemed a little nervous. They kept us hostage for over an hour. However, it felt like we were there all night with them. It was the most terrifying evening we had ever experienced. I looked over at my boss and she was crying and shaking. I would always hide my money in a prescription bottle and the boss would hide her money in the refrigerator.

Those men looked in several places and turned things upside down and could not find the money we had hidden. Then we heard the elevator coming up and someone had come to our floor to a nearby office. That was good news. Because after 6 pm, usually there is no one else in the building, except for us being the last ones to leave. We were so grateful that the two men decided to leave, and we locked the door immediately. They intended on robbing us and only left with the money they came with. My boss praised me for not telling those men where her money was. She thought I was so scared that I would tell them. She believed if it was any other lady working that night, she might have gotten us hurt and robbed. However, I was more focused on convincing them to believe me that security was coming soon to observe our place and collect the money from their massage sessions.

God was so merciful. We kept thanking God. When she was sitting on the couch crying, she said she had her hands together praying. Today, I know that my uneasiness of being in such an atmosphere was that the Holy Spirit was convicting me of sin or wrongful doing because I never felt 100% at peace nor openly joyous about what I was doing because I was ashamed and had guilt. I know now it was my grandmother's and family's prayers that were helping me to dwell on doing things that are right in the sight of God. My grandmother would always cover her entire loved ones in prayer and that God will protect us and lead us home to Him. She would pray and anoint us with olive oil if we were at her house. I am so grateful for my grandmother's prayers.

At the age of 19, I decided to save my money from what I was doing to open my first brick-and-mortar business in Upper Montclair, New Jersey. I provided deluxe services of a Swedish body massage and Deep Tissue Massage and allowed my workers to perform a topless and such only with particular clients. It appeared I was thriving and then, in a year's time, it failed. I believed it failed because I had not yet given up a work career and sinful lifestyle that was displeasing to God that I had gotten into along my journey. Sometimes I ministered to the young women who worked for me, and they would be moved to tears because God was touching their hearts.

Most of them came from very decent backgrounds and went to Church and served God before. These beautiful young ladies had realistic goals and had planned only to do this type of job temporarily. With that, we confessed that we needed to get out of this line of work and we asked God to forgive us and prayed for protection. I had prayed before or after we did wrong. We knew that God heard our prayers through facing a few horrible events that should have happened, but it didn't, and we were safe.

I tried reaching out to God to get closer to Him and to stop doing these things that weren't pleasing in His sight. But I still wanted to make a good living for my family. It was a tug of war. I did not want to lose the financial security and what I thought was fun hanging out with the ladies. I knew deep in my soul that I needed to make a change. I started working on myself and my mindset to change things. I moved out of state and made a business deal with one of the ladies that I thought was qualified to handle daily operations and become the business's new owner. Not long after I moved, I found out that she had stolen everything from me. So, I found new work quickly to try to replace the money and things in my business that she had taken from me. Meanwhile, I would pray and try to do everything else right in my life. That wasn't enough because I still couldn't let go of that type of work. One night, I was driving home to New York from New Jersey, and I fell asleep behind the wheel on the highway and the supernatural intervention of God woke me up just in time to get back on the road. I was headed to crash into a pole and trees. I was shaken and my heart was beating very fast. God let me know that it was Him that saved me. I stayed alert until I arrived home safe and sound. I knew that it was a major turning point in my life – God saved me, and I knew then I could really trust Him.

I had a serene peace about quitting that line of work and never looking back. There was a sense of peace within me, and I knew without a shadow of doubt I was going to be okay. Then I began to dwell on the fact I had other job skills before that line of work I was doing, and I can utilize those skills to grow and learn new things as well. I was hired immediately to work at Dunkin Donuts. I felt relieved and set free of my past because I had a fresh and peaceful new beginning.

I attended a new Church and rededicated my life to Christ. I went to Bible Study to learn the things of the Lord God. Not too long after that, I was witnessing for Christ. I quickly grew a love for passing out Gospel Tracts in the community and inviting others to Church because God made me free, and He wants to do the same for others. He was so gracious and gave me prophecies from strangers on the streets. One prophecy was from an evangelist walking in the neighborhood who shared the love of Christ with me. She taught me to dress modestly because I was wearing very short skirts and dresses. The next prophecy I received was at Church. God made promises to me through a visiting Prophet from California. He declared that God would bless me with a successful business, house, car, etc. if I live for Him and did what He said. I gave my resounding "Yes" to the Lord that very day. I desired to do things His way because He saved me multiple times from the things I had done and achieved the wrong way. I read Father God's Word daily for my road map. I was beginning to understand how I was created to be noble and honorable unto the Lord. Learning from my mistakes caused me to mature and never make that choice to go down an unrighteous path again.

Since then, I would go to seminars and order videotapes and books and work booklets to get into Real estate in various sectors, such as wholesaling Mobile homes and other types of property. I had applied myself to what I had studied and learned. I remember one day, my late Stepdad Mark came into the room where I was working and two of my little children were playing around me and he looked at me and said, "Keima, you are going to be very successful. Keep up the good work." That gave me hope to keep going because the responses I was receiving from the property owners were not consistent - it was a competitive market.

Holding on to God's Unchanging Hands

I became very focused on either working on one business or multiple businesses at a time: Selling Avon, saving my money to invest into Snack Vending Machines, marketing and selling weight-loss cookies, investing in a Private Label No Scalp Burn Hair relaxer system, all while being on a tight budget. I had an opportunity every year around income tax time to invest in my ideas and plans, not knowing that this plan of action (cycle) would carry on and be this way for the next 18-20 years of my life.

The business that I enjoyed the most was operating Surrogacy referral Services. For couples who could not conceive a baby on their own, I would operate a service to help match them with a potential qualified woman who can have their baby using their own sperm and eggs. Domestically, I have connected my first match. The young lady was from Colorado and contracted with a married couple from an agency I referred her to. She went through the process, and she was successfully pregnant with a baby girl for them. The baby's name was Bella. I was so excited, and I just knew that from this successful match, my business would increase and expand, and my life would change. Instead, I would only get one client who I contracted with. He was a single male in Construction from Boston, and I collected a fee. He always wanted to be a father though his past relationships did not work out. Sadly, I could never match him with a Surrogate, which grieved my heart.

I continued to work promoting my services online. A month or so went by and I received an opportunity from the same agency I had previously referred a young lady to that was a success. This larger Surrogate

24

Agency establishment offered me an opportunity to become a Surrogate and travel overseas with the owner and her daughter, who also worked for the company. The expenses for this round trip would be covered. At first, I wasn't completely sure about the opportunity because I had never been out of the country before, and I had small children at home. With that, I let them know that I would think about it. My husband at the time said he had a dream where I was on an airplane flying out of the country and he said I was so happy. This was the first confirmation. And so, I spoke to him about the opportunity and the benefits, and he thought it was an absurd or strange idea. Then I explained to him how the income could help our family, pay for my educational course, and I can get a better car. At that point, he said that I could do what I wanted to do. I knew that I did not have enough money or the kind of money I wanted to take on a trip to Europe. I was used to paying for the things I wanted myself.

So, I started getting nervous, thinking that this was completely out of the ordinary for me to do. The next thing that happened to me was an evangelist prayed with me and told me to have faith and don't doubt, but trust in God because He is leading me. Sometime after that, I received a prophetic word, "You will see success in the management of foreign or distant interests. You will also travel during this season. Be mindful of managing your emotions, for if they are allowed to interfere in your business, you will suffer losses. Keep your personal feelings out of the way and take advantage of the opportunity for success coming your way! You have the power to achieve your dreams. As long as you can get clear about exactly what you wish to do, you are guaranteed to achieve it," saith the Spirit of Grace.

Things had started lining up for this trip to take place. Surprisingly, my mother was available to babysit all my children for a week which was rare because she worked long hours and double shifts all the time, but she used her vacation days to help me. My mother was afraid that I was leaving the country for Ukraine and was crying profusely. My aunt interceded with prayer, encouraging her to realize the Lord will cover and protect me and I will have a safe return and be alright, just put her faith in Jesus.

I was prescribed various medications with 'long' needles before making the trip to prepare my body to ensure that I was ready to receive the embryo transfer right on time. I was very uncomfortable with needles, but I had mustered up the courage to inject myself in my thighs or buttocks for treatment. One side effect I experienced was my hair falling out due to the hormonal change in my body. I was disappointed, but I had come too far to stop now.

God did miraculous things during this business trip. The first miracle God gave me was when I was in Detroit, Michigan, and had some distractions and missed my flight to Amsterdam. My luggage was on that flight I had missed. I was starting to panic. I called my prayer partner, mentor, and evangelist to let her know what was going on and I asked her to pray with me. She said God said I would be alright and nothing would be missing, but I did not feel that way. She kept encouraging me to keep my mind stayed on Jesus. After waiting a little while, I was favored! A seat was available for me on another flight that was many hours apart from my original flight, but that was okay. They confirmed that my bags would be at my destination when I got there, and I would just go through the normal routine to pick them up.

The ladies and I met up and gathered at the Hotel Ukraine. Then we went on the train ride (trip) that took many hours into the next day to arrive at the Medical Clinic to get examined by the medical doctors, complete paperwork, etc. I took pictures because I had no idea that it would be the type of train similar to those in old Western or Southern movies. The train had beds and cabinets to store our things and a sliding room door. Unfortunately, I had a room with an older male stranger. I was startled and started to question the situation. Am I being tested or put in harm's way just to pray myself through or out of it? I prayed and kept my bags very close to me. He did not know how to speak English, but I was able to make signs of the Cross and prayer hands and speak about Christ Jesus with my hands and pointed him to Jesus. He was fascinated by how I looked (different from him and his race). Again, I asked one of the women I was on this trip with to take a picture of me lying down on the bed and in front of my room. I was so ecstatic about the atmosphere and the type of train I was on.

Before we got our medical procedure done at the Medical Clinic in Ukraine, I heard God's Holy Spirit voice instructing me to pray for them declaring that the procedure would be safe and successful and lay hands on their belly and declare they will be pregnant, and the babies will be healthy. I resisted at first but kept thinking that I always pray for others, and I should pray for them also. So, I got the courage to do it and prayed for myself too.

The second miracle God blessed me with was when I was waiting very long hours before I could board my next plane to the US. So, I planned for the things I would do. I ate some snacks and walked around. I also read the Bible and a few spiritual books and fell asleep at the airport. When I awoke, I saw that I still had plenty of hours before boarding my flight. So, I spoke to the Lord and said, "Ughhh, I am bored! I did all that I could do; there is nothing left for me to do." So, I began just looking through my things and thought, "Well, I will just go back to reading again or go on the internet on my cellphone."

Suddenly, a young lady came and sat next to me on my right. She was very kind and friendly. She had an accent, but I understood her clearly. She talked to me about traveling and her college and her family residing in other parts of the world. She said that she wasn't from Amsterdam, but she knew a lot about the Capital of the Neverlands. She was just visiting and had to get back home soon. Our pleasant conversation and the laughter between us continued. Therefore, I had forgotten all about my loneliness or boredom.

She said she would like to show me around Amsterdam and started naming places like the Amsterdam Canals, Bikers, Carnival, etc. I told her I couldn't do that, but I wish I could. I let her know that I have my luggage etc., and I am waiting for my next flight. She let me know that I could leave my bags with the airport attendees who were behind the counter and they would oversee them for me. She assured me that I would be back on time. Then suddenly, I felt an enormous amount of peace and trusted her. My worries and fears were gone instantly. She grabbed my hand to bring me along with her and she started skipping and I skipped along with her. We went on the train, and I started to think, "I only have a few bucks that I cannot afford to spend in Amsterdam," but I was favored and did not have to pay for anything.

The scenery in Amsterdam was so beautiful and the people were friendly and kind. The Carnival rides at the Amusement Park were amazing. I was trying to tell her that I couldn't get on the rides because three embryos were just transferred into my womb the day before. Strangely enough, she looked into my eyes, and it seemed that she knew that I could not get on any of the rides, so she didn't ask. We walked around the Park. I was full of excitement. I had asked her to take a picture of me and it appeared to me that she had no idea how to operate a cell-phone, but after showing her how to use the camera, she took my picture.

We were on our way back to get on the train. As we were entering the train station, she said she had to go, and I asked her if she was leaving right now, and she said, "yes." I said, "No, please stay with me to accompany me back to the airport." She said she couldn't, but I would be just fine. I asked her, "How do I know when to get off at the right stop?" Then she let me know what I should do. I told her if I needed help, "What would I do? Who do I talk to who knows how to speak English?" She pointed to the Police officers wearing caps and reflective yellow jackets. I looked at them and looked back at her and she was gone! She disappeared in a moment. I was shaken. I kept looking for her and could not find her anywhere. I was starting to worry and cry in the midst of so many people. Then it came to my mind to go to the Police Officers. I asked them if they spoke English and began asking the questions that I needed to have the answers to. I was safe back at the airport and still ahead of schedule. I was happy that my bags were safe and secured. I was heading back home on the airplane, and all I could do was smile and rejoice. God is good! God later revealed to me that I had encountered an Angel that He sent to me. At that point in my life, I learned to really trust in God and take Him at His word.

God blessed me with the third miracle when both ladies (mother and daughter) were pregnant and delivered healthy babies for the expecting families. I came back with more than what I had which was joy and I had the opportunity to experience God in a delight-ful way and this increased my faith to a new level. I also came back with foreign money, and I gave my mom a bill for a souvenir.

My pregnancy testing result was negative, so the embryos did not take root, and this was such a huge disappointment to me because I had to throw out my plans and start over again as to what I was going to do next. I rejoiced because the trip itself was successful. I felt led to let go of the Surrogacy business and get into something different. However, it was difficult for me to let go. And so, I continued to work and market my services until everything was no longer working for me. I exercised my faith and knew that God must have something better in store for me in my next chapter of life. Heavenly Father God is good. He has a plan.

While I am Waiting, God is Working

I had times when I would tell God, "Look, I am running out of time. I need to make money for myself and take care of my children and bills. I do appreciate the ability to get some sales from e-commerce and vehicle sales, but I need an increase because I am barely making ends meet. You need to come quickly with my wealth. Especially before these plans falter and fail again...." But year after year, I did not see wealth, more than enough nor double for my trouble for the Kingdom of God for the prosperity for my family and ministry goals. However, I saw growth in areas of my life where these experiences were humbling. I had come to mature through handling what the Heavenly Father has already blessed me with. Plus, I learned better ways to manage the funds I had coming in. I had to learn to be content because being hasty about things has proved not to be the answer. The Bible says, *"The plans of the diligent lead surely to abundance and advantage, but everyone who acts in haste comes surely to poverty (Proverbs 21:5 AMP)."*

I began to refocus and thank the Lord for all the small opportunities God has brought my way. I know that promotion comes from God, and if I am faithful over the little things, He will make me ruler over more. He will withhold no good thing from any one of His children when we walk upright.

Having the right people around me and praying warriors has been such a blessing for me. My mom and dad also encouraged me in many things that I was doing, even if they didn't understand or know exactly what it was that I was doing. I count my blessings because each person God has put in my life was very helpful to pray and inspired me to keep going and keep pursuing my oriented goals. Throughout the years and decades, I wondered if I would ever get through attack after attack and delay after delay. I was smiling and struggling, but no one knew what my heart was dealing with. Some attacks have come against me where the enemy has tried to take my finances, family, health, and so much more! Every time I took one step forward, I was pushed back about ten steps. The enemy (the devil: a liar, father of Lies, and thief who comes to steal, kill and destroy) is hard at work against me, but why? The enemy does not want me to succeed for what God has planned and purposed for my life and mostly hates that God loves His children. But God steps in right on time and will restore what the enemy has stolen with greater because of what the Lord has planned for me! I have made up my mind long ago to stand and believe the report of the Lord: "Do not fear, for I am with you; do not be afraid, for I am your God. I will strengthen you; I will surely help you; I will uphold you with My right hand of righteousness (Isaiah 41:10)." For we know that all things work together for our good to those who love God and are called according to His purpose (Romans 8:28).

As I called upon the Lord and cried out to Him, and held onto my faith, God gave me fresh strength and courage to go through the tough and unsure times in my life when I thought and when it looked like I wasn't going to make it to see the dreams and visions God gave me. Sometimes I would be up and down in my emotions. I would become disconsolate and then I would overcome that emotion and be rejoiceful. Nevertheless, God was there. He never left my side. He promises to never leave His children nor forsake us. With that, I had to take a stand and speak the oracles of God, the words of power, deliverance, healing, restoration, and life over myself and the situations I was facing. *Psalms 118:25* and *3 John 1:2* are two of the scriptures I have stood on to decree and declare by faith for my breakthrough. It reads, *"Save now. I beseech thee, O Lord: O Lord, I beseech thee, send now prosperity." "Beloved, I wish above all things that thou mayest prosper and be in health, even as thy soul prospereth."*

Now to Him (God) who is able to [carry out His purpose and] do super-abundantly more than all that we dare ask or think [infinitely beyond our greatest prayers, hopes, or dreams], according to His power that is at work within us. —Ephesians 3:20 AMP

God is so strategic. There was another season in my life when I had a divorce and I had to transition and move back to my old neighborhood in New Jersey. I did not know what I was going to do. I searched for quite a while and literally found nothing. When I quieted my own thoughts and was open to receive what God had for me, a prophecy came to the surface of my mind, and I began to reflect on the prophecy I had received some time ago that I would make a transition. I will go to the city of opportunities. The Lord is amazing! He opened a surprisingly good door of opportunity working with a relative who had an established seasonal business (five-star rated). My relative called me, letting me know that I dropped in His spirit to employ me for the position that He was looking to fill. He asked me to work part-time for Him to replace someone else He had working for Him. This job opportunity was such a blessing and right on time because that helped me get an apartment for my children and me, and I could take care of my responsibilities. Furthermore, I was able to save money for a newer vehicle.

My boss warned me early on that this was a seasonal job and that I should really think it through about financing a vehicle. Well, I wanted a newer vehicle and I kept saying God said that I would be in a new vehicle. I believed that the timing was right because I had a job and money saved and my uncle had blessed me with $1,000.00 to help put towards my vehicle.

So, I decided to use my faith to go after the vehicle I wanted. I remembered that a creative miracle happened in my past at 18 years old when I had no credit and worked off the books. I prayed and cried out to the Lord and made a vow that I would go to Church if God blessed me with the car I wholeheartedly desired. Then I received a call that they brought me my first car (Mazda 929) from NYC to Fort Lee, NJ. I paid the car off and sold it.

Glory Hallelujah! My credit score went up and then later, I messed up my credit.

For this next miracle, I went to Long Island, New York, to get my Mercedes Benz Truck and I was turned down and then was given the run around due to having no credit or little credit history. I went back home, praying and decreed and declaring that I would get my vehicle. And so, I went back again, and I insisted that this time I would not leave until I left with my vehicle. I asked a dear friend, who is like a cousin to me, to take me to the dealership because I was adamant about picking up my vehicle. On that day, I felt very good about it. I waited hours and was so glad my cousin was patient to wait there with me.

I asked the salesman to assist me to the Benz so I could sit in the truck and start it up. This time around, I did not feel excited sitting in it and the level of comfort seemed to have changed. Meanwhile, the salesman approached me and said, "Here is what we can do for you," he presented a Toyota Rav 4 SUV, with low miles. At first, I looked at him awkwardly because I thought maybe he did not hear me when I told him about the vehicle I planned to purchase. A long story short, I left the dealership with a Toyota Rav 4. I felt an overwhelming peace over my mind. I could not have been happier and in 4 years, I did not experience a single-vehicle breakdown and traveled all over the east coast. I was grateful and began to be content and thankful to the Lord. The disappointment I felt before was long gone as I faced the reality of not being able to get the vehicle I came there for. I was able to bless many people with that SUV.

After some time, my job opportunity was ended due to the company's relocation, and my position was handed over to my relative's new family. So, my income and savings were gone and that caused me to lose my vehicle to repossession, which occurred right in front of my neighbors. I was

33

embarrassed, devastated, and heartbroken. I was faced yet again with the question, "What am I going to do now?" Sometime afterward, I spoke to a woman of the faith, and I felt comforted because she explained that she lost her vehicle due to repossession and much more. It took a little while, but she was blessed to get back on her feet. She said that she knows it hurts, but I have my life and God will help me get through it — keep the faith and I will be okay.

Again, Heavenly Father God is so strategic. Before I knew it, my ex-husband had given me a car. It was not always easy to deal with him because he wanted the car back. I was wrestling with my thoughts in my mind about the cars that were given to me eventually having major break downs and I had to scramble to come up with the money to fix the problems. But no matter the circumstance, God always came through for me. I had to understand that I was blessed despite having cars with issues.

I started to get into praise and worship God and was being grateful for the good, bad, and the ugly. The Lord wants His children to count it all joy. Things could have gone much worse for me. And so, I praised Him for having a vehicle that was given to me that I did not have to pay for. God blessed me with the ability to drive and get to the places I needed to go. He sustained me in my housing situation because they were able to adjust my rent due to a loss of income. God is so, so good! It is not over until God says it is over! He has the final say. When I couldn't figure things out for myself, Father God positioned me and placed my elder relatives, my dear uncles, in my life. One at a time, I'd assist them with their personal affairs and business/property dealings yet learn from them and grow and do things like lawn upkeep, property maintenance, and even working together to fix a heater boiler. This gave me more knowledge, compassion, patience, and discipline in my life. Meanwhile, I never gave up my side hustle selling new and like-new items online and skill-building: networking in business, reviewing projects, Pitch Decks, consulting with clients, marketing, note-taking, virtual and in-person meetings, etc.

I ought to always glorify Heavenly Father God for what He blesses me and puts before me to accomplish. My one uncle would often say that they were taught to always make themselves useful. That is what I work towards regularly, and I encourage my children to do the same.

In this you rejoice, though now for a little while, if necessary, you have been grieved by various trials, so that the tested genuineness of your faith—more precious than gold that perishes though it is tested by fire—may be found to result in praise and glory and honor at the revelation of Jesus Christ. —1 Peter 1: 6-7 ESV

Miracles More Abundantly

I would have conversations with Father God throughout the years. I told Him my prayers and supplications, but not all that was on laying heavy on my heart and soul because I didn't understand a lot of what I was going through. I had a lot of questions for God. I played by the rules and worked my behind off, so why did all these failures occur in my life? Was it because I sinned and made transgressions in my first business? Was it because I went my own way and married a man you told me not to marry? Am I cursed for my disobedience? I forgave to be forgiven. I repented for doubting You, so why lasting success has not been my portion?" And so, in God's timing, He answered. I received word in Church that gave me rest. "I am forgiven. God has forgiven me. It is for God to be glorified."

A Brother from Church let me know about an Election Official Board Worker position and said I could work a few times or so every year and get paid $200-$400 for that day. At first, I was not interested because I didn't think that the job could benefit me. But God opened my eyes, and the next time I saw him, I humbly asked him how I could get started. I was blessed with that extra income and the checks arrived in the mail right on time. Not only that, but I was also able to connect with people, share God's love, and show my creative side to help others. Every day I try, and I make efforts to stay in expectancy for God to amaze me and show up and show out in my life. In *Jeremiah 33:3*, the Lord invites us to do just that. *'Call unto Me, and I will answer thee, and show thee great and mighty things, which thou knowest not.'*

I remained faithful and decided to do good in the tasks and assignments given to me to do. I recently received a surprise offer that will change my life and the lives around me in the very near future. To my astonishment, this offer was from an intelligent and great person of God and of good influence. I could have never imagined he would want to bestow such an opportunity and partner with me. Hallelujah to the Lord because Jesus The Christ is the miracle because He came that we may have life and life more abundantly. This person, who is in ministry and prestigious in the business of technology developments worldwide, has let me know that over the years, he's identified several people he'd like to work with when his ship comes in and I am one of those people. The Joint Venture partnership will provide me with a Salary for five years! He plans to come and sit down with me to discuss the JV and engage an attorney to structure it. He said he was so glad that we could work together. He has admired me and has been inspired by me for so long! I was in shock because I thought it was the other way around. I was still shocked because he is my mentor and someone I look up to.

The Holy Spirit brought back to my remembrance a contract I had with a company in my past. And so, I have shared this with this great man of God that I had a contract about 10+ years ago with a new company in Tennessee that was set to receive a large fund from investors to launch their project and I was hired to come on board as a Real Estate Senior Managing Director and the contract was for five years with the exact salary that he has offered me. When my contract was not honored, I retained an attorney to investigate the situation, the company had flunked and there was nothing I could do. With that, I said, "Look at God and how good He is!" I shouted Hallelujah! God is so good and faithful. With this new coming opportunity, I will be able to operate in Real Estate and turn my hobby into a business with this Joint Venture opportunity. God restores better than before.

We never know who is watching us and what we do, our character traits and ethics. We must keep doing good and our very best in excellence as our offering up to the Lord, sowing seeds of righteousness because we never know who Father God will touch to bless us. Scripture says, *"And let ours also learn to maintain good works for necessary uses, that they be not unfruitful."* — *Titus 3:14 KJV*

Understanding God's Way

"But he knoweth the way that I take: when he hath tried me, I shall come forth as gold." — *Job 23:10 KJV*

God knows the end from the beginning. This is my process that I endured... (the middle process before reaching my goals). I have always enjoyed being in pursuit mode as a 'Go getter.' I see an opportunity I like, go after it, and start pursuing the vision and dreams God gave me. The Lord has blessed me to help others become successful with their endeavors. I am calling those events of my life' serving in excellence.' Every so often, I would pray and always wondered when it would be my time to prosper. I also wanted to know if I was missing the mark or not understanding my divine purpose in business. God's timing is perfect. He is a right-on-time Heavenly Father.

Now I have new contacts with the right connections to conduct business. What the devil meant for evil, God has turned it around for my good. What God has for me is for me. Delay is not denial. I was just looking back at those times when I wanted to give up for good as it has been so long working on businesses that didn't thrive or rise to my expectations. I would hear from people in my life advising me to just stick with a regular or normal job. They don't know my story and cannot see where God is taking me. But through the long wait, tests and trials, and opportunities being stolen from me, God has restored back better than I had, first starting with me so I can be better prepared and groomed to receive, handle and manage the blessing.

I went to Church about a year ago and the Prophet of God called me to the altar and said, God is showing him, "It's been 18, 20 years. If God would have gave me the blessing, I would have lost it all because I wasn't ready. God says now I am ready." The race is not given to the swift, nor to the strong... but we must keep, keeping on. How will I hear the Lord say to me one day, well done thou good and faithful servant, if I haven't done what He said? Obedience is better than sacrifice. So, I have set out to do those things required of me: Writing books, speaking, ministry, business, entertainment, etc., because that is what He is leading me to do for His glory. God is rewriting my story. I am renewed in my spirit, mind, and soul as I continually seek His presence and give Him my problems.

One very vital strategy I have utilized helps me to put one foot in front of the other to keep going strong each day was meditation: meditating on God's word (Scriptural promises from the Lord), divine dreams and visions, prophecy, a Rhema Word, affirmations, wisdom from the wise, and words of encouragement from others. I would hear and see these profound things and write them down and meditate on them. This helps me keep taking small steps until I reach my goals and watch God move mightily in my situations. In a study I've read, 76% of people who wrote down the things they wanted to accomplish actually worked towards it and achieved those goals.

The Lord instructed Habakkuk to write the vision and make it plain on tablets. God declared, *"Though it tarries, wait for it,"* because He promises it *will surely come to past. For the vision is yet for an appointed time, but at the end it shall speak, and not lie: though it tarry, wait for it; because it will surely come, it will not tarry (Habakkuk 1:2-3).*

Focusing on the positive affirmations daily stirs me in the right direction for my life and I learn from my prophetic insight. I survived trauma, disappointments, hurt, and pain in my life because of God's unmerited favor and mercy and because there is safety in the multitude of counselors... *"Where there is no [wise, intelligent] guidance, the people fall [and go off course like a ship without a helm], But in the abundance of [wise and godly] counselors, there is victory."* — Proverbs 11:14 AMP

Some of these meditations are from my personal prophetic notes, dreams, etc. for encouragement, correction & reproof, and reminders to follow God's Spirit so I can stay in His will are the following:

- Do not give up. God knows I struggle with a lot of things.
- God is making my character strong.
- Persevere and have hope, my child, saith the Lord.
- Rejoice, for the Lord says, your patience will be rewarded.
- God says He has already blessed me with skills and influence for success, and I mustn't give up when it gets difficult.
- Pay closer attention because the Lord is saying I must dedicate everything I do for Him so that I can carry them out through completion.

- The Lord is saying the more I doubt Him, the less He can bless me. The more I believe in Him, the more I can bless others, and the more He can bless me.

- I am blessed with excellent intuition and sound logic and following my intuition will always lead me straight to success. Ignoring it, however, will bring the opposite results.

- The Lord said, I must not let my emotions go ahead of my mouth. I need to tame my tongue.

- Do not give full vent to my emotions.

- I will find a creative outlet in which to invest myself. God said when I awaken to my potential, I will allow my creativity to generate great wealth on my behalf.

- I am very resourceful, the Lord said.

- I know how to make things happen. I have a real fixation about knowing how to make things go and make things run. I am an excellent trader. I know how to do things in the world of commerce, yet God has given me a real skill. But it is up to me to develop that and to know that skill is with me.

- Focusing my mind on specific goals will bring many rewards, saith the Lord.

- The Lord has protected my wealth. He will continue to protect it if I faithfully obey Him. I must not let go of my faith. I will reap what I sow. The Lord wants me to sow blessings and to sow faith. The Lord wants me to be a blessing to others. I will reap these things at the right time, says the Lord.

- The Lord is saying I need to let go of my fears regarding money and obligations. When He blesses me, He will not add any trouble to it. He will be the one to provide for my needs, thus saith the Lord. The Lord knows that I suffer when debts and loans pile up.

- The fervent effectual prayer of the righteous will have miraculous results.

- God says He is my Source.
- I will experience great pain if I stubbornly hold on to people or things that are now passing out of my life.
- There is power available for whatever line of activity I choose. A position of leadership and authority is definitely extended to me, and I have begun to make very important decisions.
- I am very positive and self-assured.
- The Lord says there is a great power of healing. I have that ability because God has put the healing gifts and the healing arts right there within me. Therefore, I take note of what has been given unto me.
- I am the one that is given to a mission.

With that, I encourage every one of you reading my story to create your own meditations: any dream from the Lord, an encouraging word, gather scriptures to stand on believing God's promises and pray them over your life or circumstance. Or if there is anything that God has spoken to your heart and spirit that he wants you to know, learn or do, do it. He will never lead you wrong, only to your strength and victory.

You must submit to [correction for the purpose of] discipline; God is dealing with you as with sons; for what son is there whom his father does not discipline?
— Hebrews 12:7-11

New life begins with Christ.

I learned that I must be a character of great influence. My sequence of events and story intercepted every life around me by a choice I have made, a statement, or deed. I can help write a new chapter in someone's life and help to write affairs that happen that are good and coming from the heart of God and continue to bring others through that very door. God's people ought to have the courage and compassion to be on the mission to help the light to break through the darkness. We should continue to guide many from pitfalls. The fire we help ignite in people's lives will continue to burn. We can plant the seed in someone's life and God will nourish that seed and watch over His word to perform it.

Our story is not yet complete, we are blessed, and God's works are done through us, around us for us, and others to His amazing and powerful Glory! May our lives be the best next chapter of our lives as we rest in our Lord's arms.

My prayer for God's children is, *Lord let us never lose sight of your will and purpose for us. Strengthen us where we are weak, build us up, and make us strong, courageous, and steadfast for your Glory. Forgive us if we let fear block our faith. Let nothing take away our love for you and faith in you. Protect us from the hidden traps of the enemy. Thank you for never leaving us nor forsaking us but being with us each day in Christ Jesus's name, I pray. Amen.*

THE LESSON

I have learned so much over the years. Good jobs are available and ethical businesses that a person can work for. Then there are morally corrupt ones without integrity and jobs and businesses that God did not intend for us to be a part of but separate ourselves from the darkness of evil doers. We are deceiving ourselves by making fast money in our own way.

One of the things that I had to tune out of my life was I mustn't allow the negative talk or unconstructive criticism to get in my ear because it's like poison to me. Sometimes I didn't recognize it initially, but it is like poison. Because I would find myself doing the things I was doing before, I would no longer be doing it. Due to me allowing the poison to get in my ear. Not naturally in the physical, but in the spiritual. In the spiritual, it becomes like poison and can naturally bring on hindrances.

I had to continue to stay grounded and rooted in what I believe in who I am in the Lord. Plus, connect with those that believe and have like-minded minds. Iron sharpens Iron – that is what gives me strength, staying connected with who I am. God wants me to continue seeking His counsel and asking Him if I am in a relationship with the right person. He shakes up relationships because His purposes will prevail. As I stayed rooted in Father God, I could watch Him do miracles on my behalf. God healed my broken heart and bound up the wounds. He restored my soul. He blessed me to go through the things I went through with strength and valor. What I went through and experienced emerged a mature me and my stories can help give others hope.

Fight the good fight of faith, lay hold on eternal life, whereunto thou art also called, and hast professed a good profession before many witnesses. — 1 Timothy 6:12

CHAPTER 4

Finances

By Kimberly Moses

Money can answer a lot of our problems. If we have more money, we can do more things, whether good or bad. For instance, if you wanted to bless more people, such as buying them homes, cars, toys for Christmas, school supplies, etc., you could if you had more money. Contrarily, if you wanted to buy more drugs, alcohol, gamble, etc., you certainly could if money wasn't an issue for you. Money isn't bad and it's essential to life. We use it each month to pay our bills, buy food, put gas in our cars, and get other necessary things. However, many people have made money their god. They serve money and are obsessed with it. They go to great extremes to get more of it, such as sleeping their way to the top, killing, stealing, cheating, lying, etc. These sins occur when you love money more than you love God. *The love of money is the root of all evil (1 Timothy 6:10).*

Years ago, I blew through lots of money. I was an exotic dancer and would make $200 a night dancing in a black club. Then when I would dance in a white club, I would make $1000 a night. The next day, my home girls and I would drive out of town, eat at a restaurant, go to the mall, buy expensive things, and repeat the cycle. If I knew what I know now, I would have brought a home, purchased land, or invested the funds. When I got saved, I was tired of feeling empty inside, so I went to the strip club and cleaned out my locker and never looked back. I figured I would be okay because I had at least $10,000 in the bank, but the money quickly ran out because I was still trying to maintain my shopping, eating out, and buying flashy things.

When I got down to my last $500, worry came upon me and I cried like a baby. Even though I was newly saved, I didn't look to God yet as my provider. I met this lady and she hired me in the group home she supervised. The pay wasn't very good. I was only making $8 an hour, and many taxes came out each week. When I got my first paycheck, I went to my car and cried. "Lord, how will I survive when my check is less than $200." Miraculously, God sustained me. He put His desires in me and I no longer wanted to draw attention to myself. I didn't want to spend thousands of dollars on shopping sprees buying things that I really didn't need. I decided to go back to school and get a degree or a skill. I became a phlebotomist and my pay increased to $13 an hour, but I barely had anything left over from the check once all my monthly expenses were paid.

I knew I wanted more and wanted to live a more comfortable lifestyle, so I furthered my education and became a Registered Respiratory Therapist. Amazingly, my pay tripled, and I made close to $30 an hour. I realized that I could make more working night shifts and holidays, so I chased the dollar. When I got my first paycheck as a Respiratory Therapist, the first thing that I brought myself was a brand new Honda Pilot. Yet, I still wasn't satisfied. I wanted to become a medical doctor to make even more money.

I became a professional student. I was carnal and didn't make time for God. Slowly I backslid and the old Kim started to be resurrected. Gone was the girl who wanted to dress modestly and focus on God. The flashy Kim who needed to have the center of attention was back. I started buying things that I didn't need and ended up in thousands of dollars in debt which took me years to pay off. Money was my god even though I confessed Jesus as my Lord during this time. The more I drew away from God, the more selfish and worldly I became. I stepped out of my first marriage and lost everything.

I SURVIVED

My first marriage was hanging on by a thread. My security blanket of having lots of money in the bank was pulled from underneath me. My ex-husband and I got into a huge fight and I was kicked out of the home. Out of desperation, I called my bank and got a loan for $2,800 to live on for a few weeks. I was living in a hotel and the expenses started to increase. I was now out of money, so I went to my credit cards and maxed them out. I hired an expensive attorney and got an upscale apartment out of pride and ambition. Looking back, there really was no need for a lawyer. My ex and I could've worked things out in mediation, but due to my pride, I hired an attorney. Also, I could've lived in a more affordable place, but I wasn't willing to sacrifice for a short time until I got back on my feet.

Due to poor choices and exploding in rage, I was arrested and put on probation for three years. I was afraid to apply for a better job because I now had a criminal record and would face difficulty working in the health field. So I decided to ride things out and started seeking God. My work hours started to decrease and when I would get paid, it didn't cover all of my bills. I had to make some tough choices and downgrade. I stopped paying for expensive satellite and got Netflix for my children to watch. I could no longer afford to eat a vegan diet, so I started buying processed foods and meat. I stopped going to the salon and learned how to do my own hair and nails. All these downgrades didn't matter because I still was behind in all of my bills. I couldn't pay my utilities and my power got cut off only for one hour. I'm grateful that it was a short time and God put it on someone's heart to bless me.

After a long stressful day, I just wanted to come home and take a bath. Every time I took a bath, the Lord would speak to me. So after being in the tub for a couple of hours, I got out and hit the light switch and it was not working. I had a window to bring in natural light in my old bathroom. Since it was getting dark, I ended the bath and decided to get dressed to prepare dinner. I kept switching on the lights, and it registered that the final notice the utility company put on my front door was now in effect. I didn't know what to do, so immediately, I started praying. At that moment, I got a text. It was my friend who lived up north. She told me that she went to get her tire fixed that got damaged by some potholes, but the mechanic did it for free. She prayed and asked the Lord what she should do with the extra money and she heard the Lord say to give it to Kimberly. When she explained what happened, I told her why the Lord had instructed her to do so. She called me and we dialed the utility company on three-way. She paid the bill for me and as we waited for the lights to come on, we prayed together on the phone and worshiped. One hour later, all the lights were back on in the home.

Shortly after, things were still not better. I would call people for help with food and rent. Some people would help me and send me a couple of hundreds of dollars because I couldn't afford to pay my rent anymore. The state gave me a one-time funding to pay for my rent, but they turned me away the next time I needed help. The church only paid 1/3 of my utility bill and wouldn't cover the entire expense. My local food bank told me they could no longer help me because I could only go a set number of times and I had maxed out. I was told that I couldn't get food stamps because I made too much money, yet I was struggling and behind on my bills. Plus, my account was in the negative by hundreds of dollars.

I connected to a small church with a food bank and received a food basket every week for an entire year. I was very grateful because sometimes they would give me food that was about to be thrown away from various restaurants like Chipotle, KFC, Panera Bread, Pizza Hut, Red Lobster, and other places. During this time, I faced the added stress of my car being threatened to be towed. My tags and registration were expired and I needed to pay a few hundred dollars to get them renewed. However, it took me weeks to get the funds and I had to park my car at Walmart a few blocks away so the apartment complex I resided at wouldn't get my vehicle towed. Sometimes it would snow and rain, but I would walk many blocks to get my car, just praising and thanking God for better days. Additionally, I couldn't afford to pay my car note and car insurance anymore, so my ex-husband made the payments for me because he was a co-signer. He didn't want his credit to be destroyed. Eventually, he paid off the car even though he despised me.

To make matters worse, I got evicted. The landlord called and threatened me daily to put my stuff on the streets. I couldn't eat or sleep well. I felt like I had this dark cloud over my head. I was broken, but I knew God would come through somehow. I laid on my face all night and prayed. When I woke up, my phone rang and someone called to tell me that they had a dream about me. They informed me that they had just come into a bunch of money and knew they had to help me. They asked me what was going on and I explained. They helped find me an apartment that would allow felons to live on their premises. They wrote a check to my new landlord paying my rent off for the remainder of the year and they hired a moving company to move me into my new place. The apartment wasn't the best spot but it was affordable and smaller than the last one. I had to give away a lot of my possession because they could not fit into a one-bedroom apartment. I didn't have any furniture and when my pastor friend came to help me move into my new place, he decided to furnish my apartment.

In the meantime, God was calling me to preach His word and it was the last thing that I wanted to do. I continued to run away from the calling until one day, I was up for a promotion at one of the biggest hospital systems in the area I resided. They decided to run a background check and when they discovered I was on probation, I was terminated.

I felt so afraid. I was in my car crying and when I finished, I pulled out the Bible and my eyes ran across Psalms 56:3, "When I am afraid, I trust You." This verse put so much comfort and delight in my heart. Even though I was a single mother of two kids, I knew that I would be okay since God had just revealed that scripture to me. I was at rock bottom and knew that the only way to go was to the top. As I yielded to God, things slowly began to turn around in my life.

THE LESSON

1.   Don't worship money

For the love of money is the root of all evil (1 Timothy 6:10). Some are serving the god of mammon instead of the God of Abraham, Isaac, and Jacob. If you love money more than God, you will lose your soul. *What good is it to gain the world but lose your soul (Mark 8:36)?*

2.   You command money

God desires us to lend to many nations and not borrow (Deuteronomy 15:6). God delights in our prosperity (Psalm 35:27). When God gives us a vision, He will command the provision to fund it. Our vision, purpose, or assignment attracts provision. Once the money comes, we command it what to do or control it's function in our lives.

3.   Trust God to provide

God doesn't want us to be stressed out concerning money. He will supply all of our needs. God always has a ram in the bush or a backup plan. While you are tempted to worry, God is working behind the scenes because He already has a solution and a plan. God can sustain you and use the least likely person to bless you. Just be open to what God wants to do.

4.   Don't live above your means.

Don't try to keep up with the Jones'. It's not wise to be in debt just to put on an appearance. Is your heart pure in God's sight? God isn't impressed with our outer appearance. We must be grateful for the things we have, no matter if it's small. It's not the will of God to be stressed.

5.   You can't take money with you to eternity.

You can't take these things with you when you die. We came into this world with nothing and that's exactly how we will leave. We must invest in spiritual things and make sure we are positioned to go to heaven one day.

CHAPTER 5

Foster Care

Brittany Myers

I was born and raised in Atlanta, Georgia. Growing up, I heard and saw inappropriate things for a minor to witness. Living in the ghetto taught me many things, such as how to be tough and never back down from a fight. I know for a fact that my maternal grandmother's prayers kept me out of the grave and prison.

I grew up in a two-parent household. My mother was raised by her parents to serve God and live holy, and my father was brought up a bit differently. They did their absolute best to raise me to be a God-fearing, productive citizen.

Our family was normal until I began displaying behavioral problems. My issues became noticeable when I was in Pre-K, and those issues progressed throughout the years. My parents sought professional help for me but were turned down repeatedly. For my parents to receive support, the state would have to place me in their custody. Of course, they weren't going for that.

I SURVIVED

My peers would tease me in elementary and middle school for how I looked and talked, and outside my home, I was molested. Although my mother educated me on the difference between the good and bad touch and informed me on what steps to take if I were violated, for some odd reason, I could not muster up the courage to tell her. I internalized the abuse and became extremely angry. Due to my inability to share with my parents that I was being abused, I became a walking timebomb. Anyone who said something crazy to me or looked at me funny for too long got the business.

While in elementary and part of middle school, my parents could expect a phone call from the teacher or assistant principal. They would report that either I was fighting, yelling terrorist threats, or disrupting the class in some form or fashion. The result was usually in-house suspension or out-of-school suspension. My academic efforts were not a problem, but my behavior certainly was.

I would try my hardest to be a "good" girl, for I didn't like seeing my parents sad or upset about my behavior. I was tired of them leaving work to sit with me while I was in class due to my chaotic behavior. I remember getting angry with God, telling Him to fix me, and blaming Him for making me this way. The truth is that I couldn't help it. I wanted to do better, I TRIED, but there was a force that kept me from reaching my goal.

Transitioning to the sixth grade was a bit rough for me. Once again, I could not articulate to my parents what was going on emotionally, but it showed in my dysfunctional behavior. I went to school one day, and I was extremely anxious that day. A girl at my school didn't care for me to begin with, and that day we crossed paths and exchanged some choice words that led to a fight. The principal called the police. When the police arrived, they did their best to detain me, but I wouldn't stop. I was enraged and couldn't stop myself. At some point, I blacked out, but according to the officers, I kept trying to attack my classmate.

The officer restrained and arrested me. He made it clear that he didn't want me to go to a youth detention center, for he believed I was a good kid but was battling some underlying issues and that I needed help. I was placed in the back of the Clayton County Police car and was admitted to a psychiatric hospital.

I was there for 30 days. While I was there, my parents visited me. The look on my father's face broke my heart, for I knew he felt helpless and wanted me to come home. Although the staff, nurses, and doctors were kind to me, I had to deal with the trauma and embarrassment of it all. I knew eventually that I would have to go back home and to the school where I was arrested in front of my peers, school faculty, and staff. That was a giant pill to swallow and something I didn't want to face.

I returned home, and my parents scheduled me for ongoing therapy with a psychiatrist. It helped a little, but my home and school life were not getting any better. I still couldn't convey to them what was going on with me internally. At this point, I was angry and acting out sexually. The stress my parents endured was too much for them. They reached out for help again, and different agencies would say that they couldn't do anything since I was not committed to the state (in foster care or the juvenile justice system).

My behavior was destructive and uncontrollable at regular and alternative schools. Eventually, a decision was made for me to be sent to a psychoeducational school. At this point in my life, I didn't care anymore.

Once again, I am in a different environment where I feel different and out of place. I had no say, and I wanted my life to end.

When I turned thirteen years old (February), it wasn't exciting, nor did we celebrate it. There was a dark cloud hanging over the Myers' residence. At this time, my father was diagnosed with severe depression. In March, I was placed in the foster care system, and three days later, my father committed suicide. My case manager revealed the news to me, and for a minute, I became numb; then, the anger returned with a vengeance.

While in foster care, I was bounced around from different foster homes, group homes, youth detention centers, emergency shelters, and treatment facilities. I experienced going to various middle and high schools throughout Georgia with each move. Creating bonds with people and then cutting it short due to placement changes was even more traumatizing for me.

My case manager finally found the best foster home for me at the time. She was a lovely Christian woman who welcomed me into her home. It was familiar, for she reminded me of my grandmother, a devout believer in Christ. We went to World Changers Church International, located in Atlanta, Georgia. Things were going well until two girls at my new school began to bully me.

I tried my hardest to do well at this foster home. I went to church multiple times a week, gave my life to Christ, went to school with little to no problems, and followed the house rules. But the bullying started to get to me. I let my teachers and principal know what was happening, and nothing changed. After three months of doing things the "right" way, I snapped on the two girls who had crossed the line with me way too many times.

I was committed to the Department of Juvenile Justice system at 15 years old. The judge charged me with aggravated assault and reckless conduct. The judge didn't care that I was being bullied, but my reaction was violent. My rap sheet of being in and out of youth detention centers proved that I needed to be taught a lesson.

The judge sentenced me to one year at a long-term youth detention center and placed me on probation (16) until I was 21 years old. That was the best thing that they could do for me, for the foster care system had me moving from place to place throughout the state of Georgia, which wasn't conducive to my well-being.

While in DJJ's care, they provided stability, support, and tangible resources and connections. You would expect that a system that addresses the crimes of minors and arrest them if guilty would be a horrible entity. That's not my story. They held me accountable for my actions, listened to me, treated me like a decent human being, and included my mother throughout the entire process. It was a blessing in disguise.

Many people ask me how I overcame or survived being in foster care and the juvenile justice system. I tell them that my faith in God, my mother and grandmother's prayers, and God connecting me to the right people at the right time pulled me through. My grandmother had introduced me to Jesus through her actions. I recall her pulling out the Bible, and she turned to Psalm 23. She looked at me, and I realized she wanted me to read it at some point. I read the first sentence, and she read the next until we read the entire chapter together. That stuck with me. It taught me that go to His Word when I am unsure, confused, and without direction. That's precisely what I did and continue to do.

No matter what placement I was at, I ALWAYs had access to a Bible and worship music. That was my saving grace. When I was mad or sad, I would read the Book of Psalms. Also, I would think about the things my grandmother taught me concerning God. When I had the opportunity to call my mother and tell her that I wanted to snap on someone, she would remind me of the challenges Jesus faced, and I would calm down, for Jesus was innocent and was persecuted so that we may be free! How could I remain upset? The support I received from these two while in transition kept me grounded.

THE LESSON

In retrospect, I learned that my Heavenly Father meant what He said concerning never leaving nor forsaking me *(Deuteronomy 31:8),* that when I call on Him, He will answer *(Isaiah 65:24),* and that His plans for me are to give me a hope and future *(Jeremiah 29:11).* I thought I was alone when going through the dark times, but I was never alone. Many of my peers have either died, become incarcerated, in the streets, strung out on drugs, or have entirely lost their minds and simply floating through life.

TESTIMONY

My testimony is that God delivered me from emotionalism (ongoing), promiscuity, and violence. Everything I went through could've killed my spirit, but God kept me through it all. Not only did He save me, but He also gave me a voice. I use my voice to speak life into disadvantaged youth and those who are weary. My story reminds us that you can never cast away a person that God has anointed.

CHAPTER 6

Grief

Allena Douglas Brathwaite

<u>HOW I WAS TESTED</u>

I want to share how I was tested, tried, and survived during a challenging time in my life. I struggled with complex grief for more than 12 years. Grief is a strong, sometimes overwhelming emotion for people, regardless of whether their sadness stems from losing a loved one or a terminal diagnosis. Grief can also follow other losses such as a miscarriage or divorce or separation or learning you have a disability or severe illness, or the death of a pet; these losses can cause grief. What do you do when one of your family members dies unexpectedly? How do you deal with such intense pain.? I asked myself over and over why God and where are you? *Psalms 46:1, "God is our refuge and strength, a very present help in trouble." Hebrews 13:5 says, "Mature conversation be without covenants and be content with such things as you have for he has said I would never leave nor forsake thee."*

June 7 & 9, 2002, changed my life forever. I experienced a very intense level of heartache after my mother and my grandmother's unexpected death.

Six months before their death, I experienced a public divorce and financial devastation. I hadn't completely healed from that situation. I began working two full-time jobs and became a single parent. I tried to balance all of these new changes in my life. I thought I had done something wrong and that God was punishing me for something. On one of my sleepless nights, the Holy Spirit allowed me to read the following scriptures.

O Lord, do not forsake me; be not far from me, O my God. Come quickly to help me, O Lord, my Savior. — Psalm 38:21-22.

The idea of quiet expectation came from two verses. *Psalm 62:5* in the King James Version reads, *"My soul, wait thou only upon God; for my expectation is from Him."* And, in *Romans 8:26,* the apostle Paul says the *Holy Spirit will help us pray when we aren't sure what to say.*

The Bible says God is our comforter (*Isaiah 66:13),* but it sounded like a Christian cliché to me, saying, *"He is my Comforter."*

Yet God mercifully reached down to comfort me and met me where I was.

<u>HOW I SURVIVED</u>

I have been a dreamer and seer since I was a child. I didn't explore that gift and talent because I didn't understand my gift. As a Christian, I didn't trust my gift. I worked two jobs to support my family and provide income for my mother, son, and nephew in Louisiana. My mother had suffered two abdominal aneurysm ruptures that required surgery and two years of rehabilitation. My son and nephew lived with her and attended college at Louisiana Tech University.

My mother was scheduled for her final MD appointment and would be released to return to work soon. I worked Monday through Friday as an administrator at Best Care Home Care. It was a very stressful job; however, I worked with a great team of professionals. I had favor with the CEO and owner of the business. She became my mentor in the industry and about being a Godly woman. The Care Coordinator told me that she was concerned because I looked tired. I confided in her about the reoccurring bad dreams I had been experiencing. The dreams were of me attending a funeral in my home church. I recognized people from my childhood attending this funeral. When I went to look into the casket, I didn't see a face, and the dream would end abruptly.

She suggested that I tell our boss about my dream. I hesitated to tell my boss about my dream, fearing she would think I was crazy. Unable to shake this unnerving fear, I scheduled a meeting with my boss and told her about the dream. My boss candidly asked "Did you pray"? I said yes. She asked me, "What did the Holy Spirit say?" I told her I didn't know but had an intense feeling that I needed to go to Louisiana. She told me to go home, pray, and talk with her in the morning. I dreamed the same dream with more intensity that I needed to go to Louisiana. My boss asked me to get coverage for myself and loaned me the money for my flight and the time off.

I traveled to Fort Hood, Texas, to see my daughter. She wasn't released to travel with me. I had this intense urge to pray as I started my drive to Louisiana. I kept hearing in the spirit, "He will never leave you or forsake you." I recited Psalms 23rd over and over. As I arrived in Dallas, Texas, my sister Angela alerted me that my grandmother had been admitted to the hospital and was gravely ill. The holy spirit again spoke, *"Isaiah 66:13 as one whom his mother comforted so will I comfort you and you shall be comforted in Jerusalem."* God sent me subtle cues, but I didn't listen. I allowed fear to be a hindrance.

I arrived in Louisiana hours later and was thrilled to see my mother look healthy. After a lengthy recovery and illness, mom shared that she had an appointment to see her doctor with hopes of returning to work. We visited with my grandmother. She slept peacefully in a semi-comatose state. I was very tearful but just prayed for my grandmother. We returned home to spend a night of quality time together that night. I slept in my mother's bed just as I did when I returned from various military assignments., keeping with the same ritual as I did when we would come home from military duties.

The following day we talked as we had breakfast. Mommy kissed me on the forehead and told me she loved me and was proud of me. Mom went to visit grandmother. I met with many family members and friends. I had a great lunch with my son Darren and my nephew Joe. The boys agreed to assist their grandmother with chores, errands, and light meals sometimes. I bought the sports Jersey's that they requested.

I visited the nursing home, giving appreciation gifts to the staff and the residents and thanking them for caring for my grandmother. My friend John and I made plans to go to dinner later that evening. I went to the hospital to visit my grandmother and my mother.

As I entered my grandmother's hospital room, I noticed her flailing around in the bed and making some unintelligible noises. I immediately went to my grandmother's bedside to assist her. My mother was sleeping on a pallet next to Nana's bed on the floor. Seeing mom on the floor wasn't troubling because she made herself comfortable wherever she went. As my grandmother calmed down, I requested my mother to wake up. I said, "Mom, you will sleep through a storm or quake." When she didn't respond, I said, "You sleep so hard." I went down to shake her and noticed that she was stiff, with ashen skin color, but her skin was still warm. I started to freak out, but immediately the Holy Ghost said, "No, you are a nurse." I yelled for help and initiated CPR immediately. The nurse came in with a crash cart and team members. Two people pulled me away from my mother's chest, and the code team took over. The head nurse, Ms. Bobbie Cage, said, "Come on, Lena, let's pray."

It was difficult to pray as I watched the non-sustainable heart rhythm on the cardiac rhythm. I prayed very hard for God to intervene. God heard me; they obtained a sustainable heart rhythm and rushed my mother to ICU. I prayed and begged God to save her. I then listened to a code blue announced over the loudspeaker. I rationalized that it wasn't about my mother. Dr. Smith and the other doctor came to notify me that my mother had expired. I was devastated. I thought God had failed me, my heart ached, and I couldn't put prayers into words. The news of her death spread through our small town quickly, and there was an overwhelming amount of family and friends who supported us. Notifying my siblings of my mom's death was very challenging. I don't know how I made it through that. Reflecting on all the events, I know God kept me and sustained me. His Word says He will never leave us or forsake us. A nurse from the hospital called to express her condolences; she reassured me that they would care for my grandmother. I waited on my siblings to arrive. We were stressed not knowing if my mother had life insurance. When my sister Angela came, she started to plan my mother's funeral. I made financial arrangements to pay for the funeral by installments without insurance. Grief takes many forms and ranges of emotions. My sister was outraged and cold towards everyone. God sent us help from family and friends; however, Angela rejected every suggestion. The enemy had snuck in and tried to divide us when we needed one another the most.

On June 9th at 0200, we received a message that my grandmother had passed away peacefully in her sleep. I was utterly devastated. I ask God why?

What could I have done wrong for this to happen? We decided to bury my mother and grandmother on June 15th, 2002. We couldn't bear the thought of doing separate funerals.

We attended the funeral together as a big family and went to the church. I was surprised at the number of people who came to the funerals. There was standing room only with no room for people for all who came to honor them. I am thankful for my mother's and grandmother's legacy. We all sat together and comforted one another.

I enjoyed the eulogy that Dean Ruby Higgins spoke about my mother. I was comforted knowing that my mother had given her life to Christ and was active in the community and church. My siblings Angela, Robert, Linda, and Mark united to celebrate their legacy with our families.

My test began once I returned home to my everyday life. I returned to work and returned to my daily grind. I noticed that depression had started to creep on me. I also pulled away from God because I was angry and felt abandoned. It became tough to pray or read my Word because I thought God didn't hear me. I didn't know how to get out of that rut. I stopped attending church regularly. When I attended church, I prayed that there would be a message to help my situation. I poured myself into work, trying to parent my two boys in high school and deal with everyday life. There were times when I experienced crying spells leading to me not getting out of bed on some days. I am so thankful to my friends Susie, LaDonna, and Ica for encouraging me, pushing me, and praying for me. The Word of God says in *Matthew 18:20, "For where two or three are gathered in my name, there am I in the midst of them."*

I started to pray and ask God for help. It was still difficult because I had been listening to the enemy's lies. I had so much guilt in my heart. I believed that if I had gotten to the hospital a little earlier, my mother would still be alive. I blamed myself for her death for so long. I stayed in this state for 12 years because of this painful memory.

I talked with Colonel Lue Reeves, a hospital supervisor. She was easy to talk to, and I opened up to her telling her about my problem. She would look for me daily and talk with me. She would encourage me and tell me that she was praying for me. One day, she said, "Are you ready?" I said, "For what?" She said it is time to face your giant (trauma) to help you heal.

I made that trip to Louisiana, and it appeared to be one of the hardest things to do. I went to the Grambling State University's homecoming game, my mother's employer. What better way to honor my mother than going to the homecoming at the place that she treasured and she was the best at what she did as a nurse at Grambling. When I arrived at the airport, I secured a rental car and started my journey to Grambling. I decided to take a trip to the cemetery to visit my grandmother, grandfather, and mother. Once I arrived at the cemetery, I cried and spent time with them. I attended the game and saw a lot of alumni, classmates, and my teammates. I had a great time at the game. I explained to my friends why I stayed away so long, which led to the restoration of many friendships.

THE LESSON

I admitted to God that I was angry because He didn't hear my prayers. Why did He let so many horrible things happen to my family and me? I lost my husband, money, and possessions to divorce, my mother and grandmother were gone. What did I do so bad for all of this to happen? I continued praying and talking to God, who had never left me. I had to seek Him in the secret place and let Him heal me.

I realized God never left me. He is the author and finisher of our faith. GOD is the alpha and Omega. Ecclesiastics tells us that there is a time to live, and there's a time to die. I didn't deal with my grief and the guilt that I had in my heart. I suffered for 12 years because I didn't go through all the stages of grief. I realize that I was not in control and that it wouldn't have made a difference regardless of what I would have done that day because this was God's will. God is in control.

Everyone's grief is different. Please don't let anyone say to you that you should be over your loss by now. As a Hospice nurse, I learned that there are five stages of grief. Below are the stages and applicable scriptures to help someone on their journey with grief.

1. **Denial:** *Psalm 46*
2. **Fear:** *Psalm 62*
3. **Anger:** *Psalm 77*
4. **Guilt:** *Psalm 32*
5. **Sadness:** *Psalm 31*
6. **Hope:** *Psalm 33*
7. **Faith:** *Psalm 100*
8. **Acceptance:** *Psalm 37*
9. **Praise:** *Psalm 71*

But the Word of God's Word assures us that reign is temporary. The Lord Jesus Christ has broken in to plunder the strong man *(Mark 3:27)* and take back what is His own with resurrection power. "The last enemy to be destroyed is death *(1 Cor. 15:26)*." Hope and God's love is the reason that we can cry, and amid our tears, we can also smile. We know that our weeping is temporary, but our hope is everlasting. We are never alone. Our Lord Jesus is with us. He suffered pain and is familiar with pain" *(Isa 53:3)*, and walks beside us every step of the way. I hope that this story blesses and delivers you through your journey with grief.

CHAPTER 7

Push Through

Keeping The Faith Because God Is In The Details

By Naseska C. Young

INTRODUCTION

There is no doubt that God is the author and finisher of my faith. This is my first book collaboration. I count it an honor and privilege. When Prophetess Kimberly announced it and I saw the theme, I knew immediately that this was the perfect opportunity to give my testimony on how good God has been to me in spite of everything that has happened to me from 2020 going into 2021. From the death of my mother, unforeseen sickness, to depression that led to unhealthy debilitating weight gain, and to almost getting evicted for the second time, I knew that this was the moment to tell all. I know that my calling and place as a scribe in the kingdom of God is to write and bring Him glory now in this season and forevermore.

2020 was a year that we all can testify was a year like no other. We saw and experienced things that shook the nation and left many of us questioning our faith. From the global pandemic that has caused many to become ill and even die, to increased police encounters that led to injury and the death of so many Black males, to the looting and rioting, to the racial divide that has tried to tear this country apart by political affiliation, it was and will forever be sketched in the hearts and minds of so many. Individually, 2020 was a year that either propelled or caused stagnation by the circumstances or situations that we faced. There is a saying that the devil is in the details. I believe that it originated in the Bible with the story of Job. I will come back to this later but let me go ahead and give my testimony.

TEST

First, starting with the death of my mother. I was living in Salisbury, North Carolina, for eight years. I knew that God led me there in 2010 and I knew that it was God who led me back to my hometown of Raeford, North Carolina, in 2018.

I will never forget it. I started to get this homesick feeling that lasted for a couple of months. It stopped as soon as I decided to move. Things worked out perfectly because I knew this family that was looking for a house to rent. They rented from me until I had to finally sell my house. I never thought I would move back to Raeford, but God had other plans. My mother was diagnosed with an aggressive form of cancer one year after I returned in June 2019. She went through all the chemotherapy and radiation, but the cancer had spread to other parts of her body so quickly that the treatments were only buying her time. I knew that it was only the Holy Spirit who was using what I thought was just homesickness to bring me back to be with my family during our loss. My mother passed away one year later on September 17, 2020.

Shortly afterward, I was at home one day and had just finished eating. It was December 21, 2020, just four days before Christmas. About 10 minutes later, I felt a sharp pain in my chest that traveled down both arms. I was really scared because I had never experienced anything like this. The pain lasted only a few seconds. I immediately called 9-1-1. The dispatcher told me to take aspirin and make sure that the door was unlocked so that when the paramedics arrived they could get in just in case I was to pass out and become unconscious. When the paramedics arrived, they prepared me for transport to the hospital. Upon arrival, I was accessed and taken to triage for further evaluation. After a few hours, the doctor determined that I should be admitted because just a week before, I came to the emergency room for symptoms that almost resembled what I felt but not to this degree.

I was taken to the second floor of the hospital, which is the cardiology unit. My lab work came back and it showed that I had a small heart attack due to my Troponin level! I was in shock. Troponin is a protein found in the heart muscle that helps it contract and pump blood throughout the body. When it is out of range, it means that the heart is not functioning properly, but most notably it is a sign of a heart attack. The next day the cardiologist came in and explained to me more about what the diagnosis meant and scheduled me for a heart catheterization which showed a blockage in an artery. The surgeon determined that it wasn't severe enough to insert a coronary stent that keeps the arteries open and prevents plaque build-up. When I was released from the hospital, I was placed on several medications. I became depressed because I never imagined experiencing a heart attack. For the next few months, I lived in fear of what had happened. Thoughts constantly filled my mind of what if it happens again. Any sign of the symptoms and I would drive myself to the emergency room.

I spent days trying to figure out why this happened as I began to question whether or not I had given myself enough time to grieve the passing of my mother. I began to blame myself for my unhealthy eating habits. Now, I must admit that I have been in the medical field for over twenty years and am very knowledgeable about health and nutrition. I know what foods are healthy and what foods are unhealthy. I promised myself to stay on the straight and narrow path to eat healthier but because of anxiety and fear, I quickly relapsed. From January to September of 2021, I was unstable in my weight. I would lose at the most 10 pounds and then gain it all back. Once again, in October of 2021, I was hospitalized but not for my heart.

I was given a blood transfusion in which I received two units of blood. I was diagnosed with Anemia years ago and placed on iron supplements. Anemia is the lack of red blood cells and hemoglobin in the blood. Blood nourishes our bodies. When there are not enough red blood cells in the blood, it causes weakness and fatigue. On this particular day, I was having symptoms of tiredness and dizziness. I went to the emergency room to have my blood drawn and my red blood cell count reading was below normal. At first, I declined the blood transfusion, but the doctor and nurses reassured me that getting blood was safe because of today's advancements in medical technology. They counseled me on the impact that the Anemia was having on my heart. When there is not enough blood and oxygen flowing in the heart to circulate throughout the body, it becomes stressed and has to pump harder. Because of my new diagnosis they strongly advised me to get the transfusion to avoid another heart attack. Needless to say, this pushed me further into depression. I could hardly sleep at night and worried about the worst possible outcome.

My emotions were all over the place. One minute I was happy and the next I was sad and in despair. Not only was the passing of my mother and the sickness I was experiencing in my body heavily impacting me, but my finances were being attacked. I was in between jobs and not making the amount of money I needed to pay all my bills. I was barely getting by. I received an eviction notice from my apartment manager. This would be my second one in two years. I applied for rental assistance but was told the waiting list was six months out. I didn't know what to do.

<u>SURVIVAL</u>

As I mentioned earlier, the story of Job is the biblical reference in the Bible when the devil came to God to get permission to attack Job, for he was a righteous man who feared the Lord. He bargained with God to remove the hedge of protection from Job to prove that he would, in turn, stop loving and worshipping Him. God gave the devil permission to wreak havoc in Job's life but not touch his soul.

Job 2: 6-12 (NKJV), "⁶Now there was a day when the sons of God came to present themselves before the Lord, and Satan also came among them. ⁷ And the Lord said to Satan, "From where do you come?" So Satan answered the Lord and said, "From going to fro on the earth, and from walking back and forth on it." ⁸ Then the Lord said to Satan, "Have you considered My servant Job, that there is none like him on the earth, a blameless and upright man, one who fears God and shuns evil?" ⁹ So Satan answered the Lord and said, "Does Job fear God for nothing? ¹⁰ Have You not made a hedge around him, around his household, and around all that he has on every side? You have blessed the work of his hands, and his possessions have increased in the land. ¹¹ But now, stretch out Your hand and touch all that he has, and he will surely curse You to Your face!" ¹² And the Lord said to Satan, "Behold, all that he has is in your power; only do not lay a hand on his person." So Satan went out from the presence of the Lord."

From destroying his flock of sheep and cattle to being stricken with boils, and losing all his children to a tragic premature death, it seemed that Job had more than one reason to just give up. His friends accused him of having unconfessed sin and doing something bad and his wife advised him to curse God and die, but through it all, Job remained faithful. This is the testimony that we as believers should have here on Earth and in Heaven. We are ambassadors of Christ. *II Corinthians 5:20 (NKJV) "Now then, we are ambassadors for Christ, as though God were pleading through us: we implore you on Christ's behalf, be reconciled to God."* An ambassador is a person who has been given a special mission with the same protections and rights in another country that they would have in their own country. They are sent to make an extraordinary representation. As ambassadors of Christ, we are His representatives and our representation of Him to others should be that in the midst of life circumstances, tests, and trials to keep the faith because God is faithful.

God has a way of bringing the right people into your life at the right time to get you on the right track. One day I was watching a Facebook Live where Prophetess Kimberly was introducing four of the ministers of the Rejoice Essential podcast. One was Prophetess Stephanie Ham. She began to talk about her background in natural herbal medicines that God has given us to bring healing to our bodies. She mainly talked about Elderberry. She listed the benefits of Elderberry. It is filled with antioxidants to fight against colds, the flu, etc. She described it as being a magnifying glass that goes through your body to detect bad things that should not be there. I immediately had to call her and soon ordered a bottle of the Elderberry and other products on her website. I love the products and could tell you some amazing things that have taken place since I have been using them.

Outside of my pastors, I've never had a one-on-one relationship with a person who could give me godly and sound advice. I've heard others say that mentors are great to have. I bought this book that a friend of mine had written and in one of the chapters, she talked about how every woman needs a godly and wise woman mentor. She compared it to a Ruth and Naomi relationship. This stuck with me. I began to inquire of God and on this podcast is where I discovered Prophetess Lavonda "GiGi" Love. She talked about the "Secret Place" in Psalm 91. With everything I had been through, I knew that this was God speaking to me through her to let me know that I needed to draw closer to Him. I immediately reached out to her and she has been the mentor, the "Naomi," that I didn't have and needed and been thankful for in this season of my life. There are many levels to being in a relationship with God. In one of our conversations, she described it as standing in shallow water and then launching out into the deep water.

If you stay in the shallow water, you will find yourself lacking in trusting God to get you to where you ought to be, but when you launch out and go into the deep water, you will find yourself totally trusting God for everything. It may be scary at first when you let go and launch out into the deep water but the Holy Spirit is your Comforter and He will give you the strength to cast fear aside. She also encouraged me to be faithful in my tithes and offering. I didn't belong to a local church since I had moved back to Raeford. I was now living in the next city east of Raeford called Fayetteville. I had been praying and looking for a Bible teaching and faith-believing church. After two years, I was finally led to a church that I had passed by several times on my way home from work. I made up my mind to be faithful in my tithes and offering. The financial hardship that I struggled with is coming to a halt. A way was made for me to get the funds I needed to stop the eviction process and I am still in my apartment! I am not where I need to be financially but things are turning around for the better.

God is deeply concerned about us. We are His creation, created in His image. He is so in tune with us that He knows the number of hairs that is on our heads. *Matthew 10:30 (NKJV) "But the very hairs of your head are all numbered."* There should be no doubt that our health is important to Him. It was before Thanksgiving and I decided to go into this local business owned by a husband and wife. I had seen it several times passing by while driving on my way to the post office. They sell nutritional drinks that include teas and smoothies.

I was starting to feel better after that last episode that landed me in the hospital just a month prior but I needed a boost. The husband was serving other customers. He welcomed me in and asked me what tea or smoothie I would like to try. One of the customers said, "If I were you, I would try the cookies-n-cream smoothie. Girl, it is addicting!" She began to tell me that she had been drinking these smoothies for two years and had lost weight. She said that her diagnosis of high blood pressure and high cholesterol was reversed! I could tell that she was very happy and she looked good. After she left, I walked over to the board of pictures hanging on the wall. I noticed a before picture of her and could not believe it. The owner and his wife also had a before picture. They looked totally different! I tried the smoothie and just loved it. I felt 100% better instantly! I felt energized and within two weeks, I lost 10 pounds. The shakes helped to curve my appetite and I made an effort to make better food choices. It has not been easy because I still crave those unhealthy foods and snacks that I love so much.

I also met a lady whose flyer was hanging on the wall in a postal and delivery center in the same area where I discovered the husband and wife. I reached out to her by phone and she was just a burst of energy and enthusiasm. She is a promoter of a nutritional drink that detoxifies your body. She told me she was 70 years old! I couldn't believe it. I am making progress daily and one day, I am going to be at a healthy and desired weight. I have the victory and I decree and declare that I am healed and made whole!

LESSON

Trails come to strengthen us. Through our trials, we learn to push through and overcome. We will never know how to push through if we never go through anything. It is impossible to go through this life and not have trials or trouble. The Bible says that our days are few and filled with trouble. As it was with Job, the devil was in the details behind the attack but it was God who allowed it because He knew that through it all Job would remain faithful. Job found the strength to still love, worship, and praise God. He realized that all he was and all he had was because of God.

Job 1:20-22 (NKJV), "²⁰ Then Job arose, tore his robe, and shaved his head; and he fell to the ground and worshiped. ²¹ And he said: "Naked I came from my mother's womb, And naked shall I return there. The Lord gave, and the Lord has taken away; Blessed be the name of the Lord." ²² In all this Job did not sin nor charge God with wrong."

In the end, Job was restored and received back everything he had lost. I have learned that no matter what, to stand firm on the Word of God, praise and worship my way through. God knows who will remain faithful. The Bible describes the faithful as watchmen. A watchman is a servant whose job is to stand guard and sound the alarm when trouble is approaching. They are also prayer warriors who intercede on the behalf of others. *Luke 12:35-37 (NKJV), ³⁵ "Let your waist be girded and your lamps burning; ³⁶ and you yourselves be like men who wait for their master, when he will return from the wedding, that when he comes and knocks they may open to him immediately. ³⁷ Blessed are those servants whom the master, when he comes, will find watching."* I decree and declare that you and I are faithful servants of God and will keep our lamps burning to watch as well as pray in the midst of every test and trial. We are overcomers and will push through! In Jesus' name. Amen.

CHAPTER 8

Sickness (Cancer)

By Lavonda Gigi Love

Sickness has a way of finding us when we least expect it, but thanks be to God who giveth us the victory through Christ Jesus. I have never experienced any real health issues, even though I have a family history of different illnesses and family members going through different health challenges. I've always been healthy and only in the hospital to deliver a baby. Well, that all changed in June of 2016. I started to have excruciating pain in my left upper arm and it felt like I had fluid in it because when I would lift my arm, I could feel the fluid shift and it would be pain like no other. This went on for a while and out of nowhere, I started having pain in my chest. It got so bad that I drove myself to the hospital Emergency Department (ED) to get checked out because I had difficulty breathing. They drew labs, did an EKG, and a chest x-ray but couldn't pinpoint a diagnosis. Due to having a family history of heart problems, the ED doctor said to be on the safe side, he would admit me for further evaluation. I didn't have a primary care provider, so I fell into the care of a hospitalist who was more concerned about going on vacation than treating my complaints. He was going to discharge me home, but the cardiologist Dr. Jose Matthew was consulted to assess me, and thanks be to God, he came to see me before I was discharged. He ordered a chest CT, and that's when everything came to light. The CT scan showed a large mass growing on my left thyroid gland down into my chest.

The year before, which was 2015, I was led by Holy Spirit to do a forty-day fast. He supernaturally prepared me through the Word to be mentally able to go through and complete the assignment. He would take me into the Word and open the scriptures so clear and plain that I would cry and give God the praise for such great and awesome revelation of His Word. While all this was going on, I was fighting for the restoration of my marriage. It was me and my babies, Ariel (14) and Sir (11), going through all this with the help of God. I received a prophetic word through Prophet Martin Ricks that God said if I would be obedient, He would bless me for generations to come because of my faithfulness to Him. I cried a river of tears because I knew without a doubt that he was speaking by the Holy Ghost. I decided that I would finish strong even if it killed me, not knowing that satan was trying to do just that. God knows everything and it's imperative that we be obedient even when we don't understand the WHY. The fast started in late July and ended in early September. I was working twelve hour shifts at night as a postpartum nurse and no one knew I was fasting, not even my babies. I followed Matthew 6 about fasting to the tee because I did not want to lose my reward. After a while, people started to ask me if I was losing weight and I would say, "Stop playing and keep it moving." This way, they would see me but could not put their finger on what was really going on.

I was only allowed to drink plain water or water with fresh lemons and or limes and 100% fruit juice in moderation. Hydration was of the utmost importance for my physical body to hold up and not give out. When I was not at work or doing my mommy duties, I would be lying on my altar, spending time in His presence, being refreshed and renewed. It's of the utmost importance to stay in His presence. Even at work, I would take my breaks in the nursery to be alone and read my Word, meditate, pray, and worship. Also, I still had to do ministry and pray for others when I was so weak that I would have to prop myself up on my nightstand. God kept me and He wouldn't let go.

I SURVIVED

After the chest CT exposed the mass, they saw that I had pneumonia. I was taken aback because I couldn't understand why I had pneumonia. The mass had grown so deep in my chest that it deviated my trachea off to the right, which caused me to aspirate at some point in my sleep. I would wake up at night to a coughing spell and would cough so bad until it would wake up my children and they would come and check on me. The test also showed that the mass was abutting my carotid arteries that came off my aortic arch, significantly decreasing the upper body's oxygen supply. I would be so lethargic that I would feel like I was spacewalking. On two occasions, I went out while driving. The first time I ended up on the opposite side of the highway, but God stopped the traffic and woke me up so that I could recover myself and get back on my side of the road. The second time I went out, I woke up before going off the road into the trees. I can honestly say that I got to know my Father God in a real way because again, I didn't have anyone but Him to help me. I had to go back to my endocrinologist to get the results. He told me that the mass would have to come out and they would test it for cancer cells. No one wanted to come out and tell me that they were afraid that it might be cancerous. They talked all around that and worked on saying words to encourage me so that I wouldn't be fearful or afraid *(2 Timothy 1:7 and Ps. 23: 1-2)*.

Dr. Lubbos sent me to a surgeon for a surgical consult. When the surgeon looked had my report and CT scan, he said, "I can't do this surgery and you will most likely need a thoracic surgeon to assist because of the size of the mass or tumor." Bottom line, he was telling me that they would most likely have to open my chest the way they do for patients who have bypass surgery on their hearts. By this time, I had gone through so many tests and trials until nothing he was saying phased me. I knew God had me because whatever He asked of me, I gave it to Him. *Psalms 119:71* says that it was good for me to be afflicted, that I might learn His ways. *Luke 8: 43-48* talks about the woman with the issue of blood and how she spent all her money going from doctor to doctor, but no one could cure her. I went to serval doctors and sickness has a way of depleting your funds because it can get expensive. I was then sent to see a surgeon in Alexandria, Louisiana, who sent me to see a thoracic surgeon. He gave me a price of what his fees would be and there was a guarantee that he would even need to assist in my surgery, but just for him to be there would cost me thousands of dollars. After talking to the second surgeon again, he was trying to convince me that I wasn't truly having any issues from the mass and that the CT scan report was not accurate. When a doctor is cocky and too full of himself, I run. I was then referred to Tulane Medical in NOLA. That was a disaster. Finally, I went to MD Anderson Cancer Center in Houston and on December 6, 2016, I had the surgery and God showed up and showed out. I didn't lose my voice and thanks be to God, it didn't change. The enemy lost again. HalleluYah!!!!!

THE LESSON

1. Always obey God when He speaks, whether you understand the why or not *(1 Samuel 15:22)*. Even when the fire has been turned up in your life, know that God will never allow you to go through alone *(Daniel 3:8-25)*. Even the enemy recognizes Jesus when He's on the scene. Just rest in the fact that the Son of Man is with you.
2. Stand even if you are standing alone *(Ephesians 6: 10-18)*.
3. Your faith will make you whole *(Hebrews 11: 1)*.

4. Trusting in God makes Him proud of us. The Holy Spirit is searching the earth, looking for faith. Not perfect people, but FAITH.

5. Sickness is not of God, but the devil *(Isaiah 53: 1-5).*

6. I learned that I'm an overcomer and that the Word of God is true *(1 John 4:4 AMP).*

7. Praise and worship, fasting, and prayer are truly the weapons of the saints *(Psalms 34:1 NKJV).*

CHAPTER 9

Sickness (COVID)

Allena Douglas Brathwaite

The COVID Pandemic is something that I thought I never see in my lifetime. The world has been in upheaval since COVID-19 was unleashed on us. This disease process was unknown, and the world didn't know what to do or how to treat this disease. Because of the strange aspects of COVID-19, and I am in the category with underlying health issues, I went home to telework. My husband is a security guard at the hospital, daily working as a frontline worker. As Covid 19 came on the scene, we listened to the news daily, CDC guidance on staying healthy, and work guidance. We stocked up on water, food, cleaning supplies, and toilet paper. I think we became obsessed with cleaning. My husband would take off his uniform in the garage and spray himself down with Lysol before entering the house. My sister, who lives with us, worked outside of the home and took necessary precautions.

I continued to work daily with an astronomical patient caseload. I barely left my computer most days except to go to the bathroom or stretch my legs. During my break times, I prayed hard for the pandemic, a cure, and protection for what was to come. I was somewhat sad as I listened to the news daily and briefings from the hospital. It seemed like the Coronavirus Pandemic had taken over our whole life. There seemed to be no focus on other vital things in the world or our daily lives.

As time went along, we planned for Christmas as we usually did. However, things weren't normal at all. We were cautious about doing all of our shopping. We sent gift cards to all our grandchildren and children. We shopped during off-peak hours to have less contact with vast amounts of shoppers and people. Because of the conspiracy theorists, politics, and personal liberties, people didn't heed the recommended precautions such as wearing masks, sanitizing, and gloves. I was excited that my daughter Erica, her husband Ferman, and four grandsons would spend Christmas with us this year.

On December 17, 2020, my husband called me at 0240 am. When I looked at the clock, I said he had his times mixed up. I thought he was calling me to wake me up for work, as he does daily.

So he and I talked a little. He then said, "Baby, I am sick. "I got checked out, and they said I have coronavirus." I immediately began to pray. Fear tried to set in. I started to think about the eight cousins who died related to this horrible disease. I started declaring scriptures and prayers to overcome the fear I felt in my heart. I prepared for my husband to quarantine in the room and stay in my office, where I worked daily.

HOW I SURVIVED

When he came home, I had the room set up for him. I had all my medical accessories set up because I would take care of him between seeing my patients virtually in my office. My husband Jose looked worn but mostly afraid. I anointed his head and body with anointing oil. *James 5:14 (KJV) states: "Is any sick among you? Let him call for the elders of the church, and let them pray over him, with oil in the name of the Lord."*

I immediately decree and declare *Psalms 118:17(KJV)* over him. *"I shall not die but live and declare the works of the Lord."* I notified my boss that my husband tested positive for COVID 19. I called my sister and told her that Jose's test results were positive and that we needed to get tested. My initial test results were negative. However, my sister's results were positive. I told her that she would need to quarantine.

Initially, I was overwhelmed and afraid. I reminded myself that I was a nurse, and with God's help, I would get them through this pandemic. My regimen included taking their temperatures at 0500 and subsequently. Every 3-4 hours, I offered water, Gatorade, or juice. I administered over-the-counter Dayquil or Mucinex. I ensured that they had three meals a day even if they didn't want to eat. I continued to work providing virtual appointments to my patients daily. My day began at 0400 am, or 0500 am, praying and reading my word. I cleaned my house multiple times during the day with Pine-sol, Fabuloso, and Lysol Cleaner. I would check at 0600. Take water and juice into the rooms. I would insist that they eat a small breakfast. I showered and got ready to start my workday.

I remember talking to the children about Jose and Angela. We had to cancel Christmas. We all were so disappointed because we hadn't seen each other for a long time. My daughter and family live in Oklahoma at the military base.

Everyone was fearful and afraid for me because of my significant health issues, and they were worried if I got COVID 19, it would kill me. In about four days, I became weary, tired, and overwhelmed. I would ask God, "Please don't allow me to become ill. I need to take care of my family." One night, my husband got out of bed and asked me to come into the room. He said, "Please pray with me. I had a dream. I felt the life leave my body, and I was staring down at myself." He was frail, and his fever was 103. I gave him medication and fluids. I began to pray. I asked God not to take my husband. In the book "*I Almost Died*," I remembered that there were 100 declarations to cancel death. I decreed and declared those 100 declarations over my husband as he drifted off to sleep.

My husband and sister were still ill, but I noticed they both started to get a little stronger. I was praying with the late Prophetess Stephanie Ham, the creator of Elderberry Blast. I ordered three bottles of this immune buster for us, adding it to our daily regimen of vitamins and medications.

We received prayer from many people, friends far and near, and neighbors. A few people bought meals, juice, and water and placed them at our door. I used Door dash to deliver meals and Instacart to deliver groceries and medications. Those prayers and acts of kindness lifted my family and me, sustained us, and strengthened us. On December 22, 2020, I became ill. My husband apologized and had so much guilt because he felt as though he had made me sick. I notified my boss and told him I was ill and would obtain another Covid-19 test. I saw my patients on December 23, 2020. I later received the news that I was COVID-19 positive.

My bout with COVID-19 was severe. I experienced fevers, coughing, body aches, headaches, and gastrointestinal problems. My gastroenterologist delayed surgery for six months. I notified my neurologist because of the intensity of the headaches. My sister and I went to Urgent Care because of our battle with COVID on January 4, 2021. We were retested about the 10-12th of January 2021 and were released to go back to work. My sister faced unemployment because she worked for a temp agency. My sister tried to get unemployment but was denied. My husband and I covered her bills until February. We paid her storage bill through January. My sister lost many of her worldly possessions in her storage because she didn't pay them before February 08, 2021. She had just started working again and planned to pay them when she received her pay. This is an example of people's evil hearts, greed, and not being compassionate.

I went to the hospital where I worked to receive medical treatment. I noticed that people looked at me strangely and walked over to the other side if they saw me coming toward them. This was very uncomfortable, making me sad and upset. My husband and I were informed that another employee called another employee, revealing that my husband had COVID-19. That employee went floor to floor in the hospital, telling others that my husband and I had COVID-19. Adding insult to injury, she eluded that he had been coughing for two weeks and that he had probably infected everyone. My husband takes Lotensin for his blood pressure and has a chronic cough related to the medicine. I complained to the patient advocate, and he reported the incident. A few days later, I received a call from the DCCS. She asked me for the names of the employees that breached HIPPA. I didn't know their names because I didn't work with them; my husband did. I told her I didn't want to harm those employees, but this was a HIPPA violation. She asked me if she may look in my chart, and I said yes. I never heard from the DCCS again.

I faced multiple challenges with my health after the initial battle with COVID-19. I am considered a COVID-19 long hauler. I have struggled with my health issues, but my faith makes me believe that God is and will heal me completely. My family and I survived because God had a plan for our lives. I wasn't covered under the Cares Act and had to take most of my time without pay. This was a very expensive illness because our meals, groceries, and medications were delivered. I am thankful that God has faithfully provided for us, and we didn't suffer financially. I thank God for his grace and mercy. We are still here.

THE LESSON

Despite the disproportionate death rate from COVID-19 among African Americans, we survived. We also had pre-existing medical conditions that made us more susceptible to Covid-19 with a certain amount of lethality if we were infected. I heard this signature scripture quoted over and over. *2 Chronicles 7:14, "If my people who are called by my name, shall humble themselves and pray, seek my face, and turn from their wicked ways; then I will hear from heaven and forgive their sin, and will heal the land."* I read *2 Chronicles 7:13. "If I shut up heaven that there be no rain, or I command the locust to devour the land, or I send pestilence among my people."* I believe that *2 Chronicles 7:13* explains our pandemic.

Covid is real. It is possible to survive with God's grace and mercy. No matter what we go through, God continues to let us know He is with us. You can't give up. You must fight.

My prayer life reading of the word became intense, but I must admit that this experience strengthened my Christian walk and took me to another level in ministry. We returned to work after our battle with COVID-19. Our recovery has increased our faith and let us know that God answered our prayers.

CHAPTER 10

Sickness (COVID)

By *Kimberly Moses*

In 2019, the world changed with a deadly new coronavirus or COVID-19 emerged. I believe that I had Covid more than once and the first time that I had it, I wasn't quite sure exactly how I was sick, but I knew it was more than a cold or the flu. Since the virus was brand new, there weren't any tests available and testing wasn't accessible. I was severely sick. It all started when my husband and I planned to move out of the rural area and live in the city. We were tired of living near farm land where deer, rodents, pests, and lack of decent internet service were the norm. I was weary from traveling to the city whenever I wanted to do a video for my ministry. I would have to drive in a McDonald's or Aldi's parking lot and sit in the car to go LIVE on Facebook or YouTube. When it would rain, I would have to try to overtalk the loud noise of the beating rain drops hitting my vehicle. I had no privacy and people would stare in my car as I preached and prayed.

I was able to find an affordable apartment but had hoped to buy our first home. My husband and I moved into our new place and we talked with various realtors. We knew my children were coming back from Japan to live with us within a few months, so we wanted to have enough room for them to stay. They had been living with their father for two years. One of the realtors was extremely nice and she went above and beyond to find something within our budget. When she showed us some properties, I started to feel sick. My nose was stuffy and I felt feverish. Later that night, I was extremely fatigued and I developed a cough. I slept for almost ten hours and didn't want to get out of bed.

My husband was very concerned about me, so he made sure I stayed hydrated. I didn't have much of an appetite, but I managed to eat a small amount. I could not stop coughing. My coughs were dry and deep. My husband brought me a lot of cough syrup. I still had to do ministry work, so I would drink a bunch of cough syrup and get on camera. Sometimes, I would press through the cough when I felt it coming on or ended the video early. After a while, I stopped getting on camera and started to do more recordings on the phone. I knew that I could always mute myself when I needed to cough. I drank a lot of Theraflu, hot tea, and even exercised. This cough lasted three months.

One day I was lying in bed and I heard the devil tell me I would die. I had to pray with everything within me to rebuke him and encourage myself that I would live because God promised me so many things that hadn't come to pass yet. I told God to let me live and heal me because I trusted Him and I didn't have any medical insurance to go to the doctor. At the time, my husband and I couldn't afford insurance and weren't able to go to the doctor for a few years. Over a few weeks, my strength returned, and the cough went away.

My husband and I knew that I had Covid because it was all over the news and I had most of the symptoms even though I wasn't diagnosed. My husband didn't get as sick as me for some strange reason, but he did have a sore throat and cough.

The second time I had COVID-19, I was diagnosed or tested positive in April 2021. My husband was working many night shifts and there were outbreaks on his job. Many departments were empty, so he had to work overtime due to a lack of staff. As a result, he contracted Coronavirus. He didn't know he had it at first, but I knew something was wrong when he stayed in bed for a week. On Monday, he slept most of the day. I figured that he had been working a lot, so he was just tired from work. On Tuesday, I expected him to get up and do some work around the home since it was his day off, but he slept most of the day. I had to wake him to make him eat something but he barely touched his food. My husband loves to eat, so this was a red flag. On Wednesday, he was scheduled to work but complained about feeling fatigued. He managed to pull himself together, but he couldn't complete his shift. I had to pick him up so he could get back in bed.

I told my husband to go to the doctor, but he refused. Sometimes men can be stubborn, but I didn't press the issue. I just prayed. He wasn't scheduled to work on Thursday, so he spent his entire day sleeping. He just told me that he wanted to rest. Once again, he barely ate or drank. On Friday, he called out of work and he did not feel better even being in bed all day. I began to fuss at him, but he didn't listen so I called his mother and sister to express my concerns. His mother came to the house and said, "You need to get tested because you might have covid." My husband didn't agree, and I told him I felt fine and didn't have any symptoms. His mother wasn't in agreement and she took the necessary precautions such as wearing a mask and social distancing when she came over to the house. She wasn't worried about contracting the virus because she was vaccinated.

My husband was booked to do a wedding the next day, but he still felt weak. He was the photographer and I was his assistant. I helped shoot videos and even took photos. Eventually, I did everything myself because my husband felt weak and went to the car to rest. I am not skilled in photography, but I pretended to know what I was doing. My husband gave me a quick lesson before going to the car, so the photos came out beautifully by the grace of God. I had to break down all the photography and videography equipment by myself because my husband was still feeling bad.

On the drive home, I talked to my husband again about going to the doctor. He told me that he would go to the emergency room if he didn't feel better tomorrow. He was scheduled to work on Sunday, but he could barely move or walk. He was sweating profusely as he dressed and his legs were weak. As we walked to the car so he could go to work, he was walked slowly as if he was in pain. As we drove to his job, he closed his eyes and tried to go back to sleep. I begged him not to go to work but to the emergency room instead. I told my husband that I would wait in the parking lot if he changed his mind about working. He didn't listen, so as he got out of the car and started walking through the parking lot, he started sweating profusely and his heart raced. He managed to get into the door and ran into his supervisor. He informed his supervisor that he wasn't feeling well and was going to go to the emergency room. His supervisor agreed because he didn't look the best.

My husband called me and told me to take him to the emergency room. I was glad. I picked up my husband and prayed that all would be well as we drove to the hospital. When we arrived, my husband could not walk straight and I had to help hold him up and check him in because he had no strength. When he was seen, the nurses and doctors ran tests, then once the results came back, they told my husband that he did have Covid. They prescribed him some steroids and some medication that looked like pearls to help his cough.

I SURVIVED

Over the next few days, my husband started to feel better, but now I started to feel bad. I scheduled a test at CVS to get tested for COVID and it came back positive. The cough that I finally got rid of came back with a vengeance. However, this time was different because I had symptoms I didn't have the first time. My head was pounding, and I felt like I got run over by a truck. My entire body hurt and I could feel the aches deep down in my bones. I had a fever and chills. I didn't know if I wanted to put covers on me or not because I was freezing but hot at the same time. I barely had strength and now I was the one sleeping the entire day.

I could not do my ministry schedule, so some intercessors stepped up and did everything until I was able to come back. I could barely talk on the phone, so there was no way I could pray for others when I could barely pray for myself. It took a couple of weeks for my voice to get stronger. Since I didn't have much energy to cook, my parents, sister, and mother-in-law all dropped off or ordered groceries for us. Having food that was already prepared or snacks was a blessing because eating helped me stay nourished.

I felt like I was dying and I thought I was not going to make it many times. I felt death was near and once again, I had to pray that I would live to declare the works of the Lord. Sometimes my prayer was, "Lord, help me Jesus!" Then I would close my eyes and drift off into a deep sleep. When I informed people who were a part of my ministry that I had Covid, they prayed for me around the clock and within a few days, I was on the road to recovery. I am very fortunate to be alive and I thank God daily for life because I gained a great appreciation for it. We lost a lot of good people to

Covid-19, but God didn't allow me to die. I believe it's because I still have more work to do on the earth.

THE LESSON

1.   Trust God for Protection

These are uncertain times during the pandemic and the news is getting crazier. We see biblical prophecy being fulfilled and know that Jesus' return is closer than ever. The best thing we can do is trust God to protect us and stay in His will. God's anointing will protect us. I believe the anointing on my life kept me when the enemy tried to kill me.

2.   Encourage Yourself With Your Prophecy

You must encourage yourself with prophecy when you are at a fork in the road or in the valley of decisions. Think and pray for everything that God has ever spoken concerning you. Bring those prophecies back to the Lord's remembrance. As death was knocking on my door, I said, "Lord, the prophecy you gave me hasn't happened yet. I can't die." At that moment, I had hope and the will power to fight the enemy off. When the devil whispered to me that I would die, I declared God's Word and prophecies over my destiny.

3.   Listen To Your Spouse

God gives us spouses to love, encourage, support, help, and cover us. We are our spouses' intercessors and can pray for deliverance over them. If my husband had never listened to me, he would not be here today. God does speak through our spouses if He needs to. God used a donkey to speak a message *(Numbers 22:21-39)*. Our spouses are not our enemies. God has placed us with our spouses for purpose.

4.   Don't Think You Are Invincible.

We have lost a lot of people to Covid-19 because they thought they were invincible and that they were too young to get sick. They didn't wear their mask, practice social distancing, and continued to live recklessly. Some did not get vaccinated. As a result, many perished and wished they would have done things differently. We only get one life on earth and we must be a good steward over it. Death doesn't discriminate against age, sex, economic status, race, etc.

5.   Use Wisdom

We don't have to die prematurely if we use wisdom. If you lack wisdom, ask God for it because He promised to give it out generously without reproach *(James 1:5)*. Foolish choices equal deadly consequences. If you feel pain in your body or notice an abnormal routine, pay careful attention because it could be life or death. Don't brush off how you feel or what you discern because it could be a window or an opportunity to get lifesaving help.

CHAPTER 11

The Great Escape

By Annette Stadmire

At the age of eight, I learned to understand who God is. I would listen to my mother sing songs of praise to the name of God with joy. She always sang acapella; her voice was loud and strong akin to Mahalia Jackson. I didn't know anything concerning the Bible at the time, but we had a large Bible that stayed open on the *23rd Psalms*. This Bible had the names of relatives listed as a family tree from all sides of the family. We had a big, beautiful picture on the wall of the man my mother calls Jesus. I remember some relatives had pictures in their homes as well, along with pictures of Martin Luther King Jr. People would refer to him as a great man of God. I was told my grandfather was a preacher who had passed away when I was four.

Many knew him as a praying man of God. So, my mother was surrounded by prayer. I was taught that if you were worried about anything, talk to God about it. Even though I did not understand how to talk to God, I still would search for a place to be alone to speak with Him. A white sandy road ran along my house near a railroad track, and there was no traffic on this road. This place had become my secret place to go, where I would often talk with God.

I would kneel and then start my prayer with "I know you hear me" as I looked up in the sky because I thought that is where He lived. I had so many questions and I wanted answers. I would pour out my deepest thoughts to Him. With tears of sorrow, I shared only with Him. I would always wait for Him to show me a sign. I wanted Him to keep my family safe and I always would compare my surroundings with what my relatives had and what I wanted for my mom.

I never expressed what we did not have to my mom because I didn't want to add to her problems. My mother was always working hard, making sure she supported us. When I started going to church, I felt so at peace. It was my escape from how I was living. I would gather around the other kids my age, whom I soon would learn were going through some of the same issues as I did. We were always in church, sometimes for hours, which I did not mind. Prayer was always the start of every service and the pastor's wife was in charge.

I loved the way she prayed, addressing the needs of the families. The pastor's wife was a beautiful woman with no children, but her husband, the pastor had children of his own from his 1st wife. He was a widow, and his children were adults. The pastor's wife would always have different children stay the weekends at their home. I really didn't like going because the pastor would cook garlic in everything he prepared, and the smell would cause me to have awful headaches and feel sick.

Sitting outside for fresh air did not help because the smell would echo through outside and the pastor would always smell like garlic, even in church. My sister and I would always go together to stay with them. The pastor's wife was the only person my mother allowed us to stay with at times. We were so happy to return home each time we went. As time went by, being involved in singing in a choir and traveling to multiple churches for dedicated events, we were always busy. But I still found time to go and pray secretly on the white sandy road.

Each time I prayed, I would familiarize myself with His presence. He was a friend whom I trusted. Sometimes I would feel a cold breeze or chills on my arm or the side of my face but did not understand what it was. I had developed a bond with Him and felt He loved me. Things around me had begun to change. My mother would visit the elderly Christian women in our neighborhood who were widows. I would often help them clean their houses or whatever they needed me to do as my mother talked to them. My mom reassures me that God would bless me for serving the elderly.

The women in the church would have a get-together with the pastor's wife and go gleaning, which was all day. During this time, they would share the gospel of Jesus Christ and ask for donations for a building project. Soon after, many of the church women could not continue the gleaning anymore. The following year someone had donated a used car to the pastor's wife so that she could do missionary work for the church. Some of the members tried to teach her how to drive but failed with repeated attempts.

The rumor was, "Do not ride with her. She is a bad driver and drives too slow." Back in those days living in the country, some did not have a driver's license. The jokes and the laughter about her driving ability spread in the community quickly. I am sure she knew the members made excuses not to get in the car with her.

But this did not stop her excitement to visit those who were sick. Early one morning, the pastor's wife came knocking on our door and asked my mom if my sister and me could go with her to visit the sick. My mother agreed with it, but my sister was always the type of child that expressed her feelings. She was not going but I agreed anyway, which gave me time not to be at home. I loved my mom and siblings and often worried about their safety when I was not around.

My stepfather was an evil man that would take his anger out on me when my mother was not around. I thought he really hated me because if there were any arguments with me being involved, I was always blamed and never allowed to explain even if I was right. It did not matter to him. He would always react violently toward me with a punch so hard in the arms or slapping me in the face.

No one dared to say a word to him in fear that he might have decided to hit them. I soon learned to stay out of sight and avoid confrontation with anyone. I held my thoughts within myself in silence. It became my best weapon. So, for many years I never held a conversation with my step-father. If he asked me a question, I would always respond with quick and direct words. As I traveled with the pastor's wife, I often wondered if she knew anything. She never asked me any questions about home or how my summer was. She was always singing and focused on the road.

I paid close attention as she drove slowly, doing 10 – 15 mph. These were summer months which were extremely hot with heat as 95-degree weather. The car had no AC, but she had church fans with Martin Luther King's picture on the front and the back that advertised the funeral home. She would fan herself and continue singing. On one of the trips, starting our day as usual, we were headed to visit the mother of the church.

We were on a single-lane road. As she drove, the loud sounds of a siren with flashing light were behind her. It was an ambulance waiting to pass.

She never panicked or even tried to move over. I was going to say something but thought, "Why she won't just pull over in the grass," but she completely ignored them. Finally, the ambulance driver quickly went on the side of her, into the grass to get by. I knew they had to be terribly angry with her. Afterward, I kept looking at her, wondering if she was okay. By the time we arrived at our destination, we were soaked in sweat from the heat.

She always wore long white dresses and a white hat. She had so much joy going into the homes giving God praise and thanks. She carried the presence of peace with her, and I would feel it as well. When she entered each of the women's homes, she greeted them by their titles given to them in the church. If they were a sister, mother, evangelist, missionary, or pastor, she always addressed each with proper respect with their calling in ministry. Most of the homes had only a fan blowing stifling air, so I sat as close to the fan only to breathe in hot air. The pastor's wife never complained about how hot it was.

She was on a mission to pray for their needs and speak the promises of God. This was the start of God preparing me for missionary work. I did not know it at that time, but God had a plan. He was positioning me for work in the ministry at an early age.

<u>TESTED</u>

After many summers traveling with the pastor's wife, I learned that God used her in many unexplainable ways. But I listened each time she prayed for healing and sometimes finances. She had confidence in her prayer that God would answer her. Weeks later, the people would return to church. They gave testimonies on how God healed them or paid bills unexpectedly. As I was getting much older, developing into a young woman, I wanted more of God and wanted to understand the mystery of Him. At the age of 13, I would have severe stomachaches.

My mother had provided me with medications that did not have any effect. So, I went to the doctor and my diagnosis was that I had stomach ulcers. So, the doctor wanted to know if there was a reason I was worried. I certainly was not going to say anything to him about my thoughts. I was a child that kept my feelings to myself, although my mom kept my sister and me safe as much as she could and felt we would be okay if we stayed home or went to church on days of service.

She worked a lot of hours at night and day. So, men in the neighborhood would comment about how I looked and stared at me when I passed by when she wasn't around, which made me angry and uncomfortable. I kept my distance. My sister and me stayed in church. When my mom was working, we would always stay together, never leaving each other's side. So, we were unaware of the intentions of a close family member that took me far away from home against my will. My sister argued for him to take someone else. I said, "I do not want to go." But he insisted, "You are going to help me with something."

I did not believe him and at that time, my stomach began to hurt because I knew he was going to rape me and kill me. I cried, sobbed, and shook. I was afraid and repeatedly asked Jesus for His help as this man took me down in a deeply wooded area. He would stop as if he were puzzled several times, so he continued to drive. All I could think about was my family if he killed me.

My sister knew he had taken me. Back in those days, most people did not have phones, so my sister went and told other family members what had happened. They could not look for me because they did not have anywhere to start. I was a child up against a big man. When he came to a complete stop, I jumped out of the vehicle with all my strength and ran through trees of wood for miles. I could hear his vehicle roaring loudly, trying to find me. I was cut upon every part of my body, running as fast as I could while bleeding.

I had lost my shoes, so the cuts on my feet were bleeding. I tried to hide at times to catch my breath, waiting for his vehicle to pass me. My body became so weak from running. My legs collapsed and I could not move anymore. He eventually caught me hiding and came toward me with fear on his face as if I was a ghost. He demanded me to get in the vehicle. I felt lifeless trying to walk. I did not know at that point what he was going to do to me. I had no strength left in me, only tears. I got in the vehicle as close as possible, leaning against the door, but I continued praying, never letting the words Jesus leave my lips. Surprisingly he drove me back home and left.

My sister knew when I left that I was going to be killed. I remember my mom would say prayers like, "Lord, watch over my children and keep them safe and let no one take their lives and do not let them take anyone's life either." And because of the prayers I started as a child of God, I knew He saved my life. I went inside the house with my sister. I was unable to speak, petrified of the events that had happened. I just wanted my mom, who was still at work.

She had no idea of what I had just experienced. Waiting for her felt like hours. My sister stayed hulled with me in bed. I could not understand why this happened to me. I felt like I was still running as I looked at my body with so many cuts that it began to burn and hurt. I had fallen asleep with my sister from exhaustion. I did not see my mom until the next morning. When she heard what happened to me, she was horrified and outraged, so she confronted the perpetrator. She screamed, asking him, "What did you do to my daughter?" He repeatedly said, "I did not do anything to her.

Take her to the doctor." I hated every word that came out of his mouth and the sight of him made me wish he would die. I was numb and shaking uncontrollably, reliving it all over again, having a mental breakdown from it. Living on farmland in the country, to report a rape, you had to actually be raped for the police to get involved. So, nothing could be done to this man.

After refusing, my mom tried to comfort me, reassuring me that she loved me and she would protect all her children. She made plans with our church mother to watch out for us when she worked. My world had changed. I grew, silently holding my feelings within. I had developed the feeling of not liking myself. I always tried to hide my body and afraid men were watching me. Therefore, as a young girl in my teens, I developed several stomach ulcers over an extended period.

I was extremely sensitive about everything, and I prayed even more because of what happened to me. As I was getting older, I loved God more than anything. I truly knew He was real, and He heard my cry when I was in trouble, and He rescued me. I tried to block out those memories and I never spoke about them to anyone again because of shame. I walked around with so much fear. I often wonder if there were other children like me that endured this type of trauma. But I thank God I wasn't raped. I enjoyed the fellowship with others in the church. Life was school and church, even though things around me seemed to have changed. When I was nine, I gave my life to the Lord.

As a church girl, you were considered saved by inviting Jesus into your heart, and you were expected to live holy and sustain from having sex until marriage. The young people in the church supported each other. We weren't allowed to date anyone outside of our beliefs. When dating, you had to be equally yoked, meaning having the same beliefs and principles as the Bible said. We weren't allowed to listen to secular music, wear pants or certain hairstyles that were considered worldly fashions that went against God's standards for how a Christian should dress.

As time went by, most of the young women had entered high school and the attraction to boys grew. They could not maintain themselves to keep from being sexually active, which resulted in secret pregnancies and abortions. Some of the families in the church were scorned and embarrassed for not having control over their daughters. I quickly learned that what they preached about in church was not the lifestyle everyone was committed to living outside of the church.

My eyes became more open as I continued in my prayers. The church had become less interesting, but my sister and I continued to go despite rumors. My mother was interested in other television ministries and stayed away from the gossip. As I matured and saw disturbing problems between families in the church, it was already a division inside the church. The men didn't sit with their wives and the women and children sat together. The church members felt like the men would be distracted from hearing the Word of God. I experienced my first healing along with my mom praying with me. The ulcers I had were gone after two years of praying.

I thanked God that He showed me His glory each time I had struggled with issues and His love. The last summer I traveled with the pastor's wife, I was about 15 years old. I joined the chorus in school. I didn't let anyone know at that time because they sang mostly classical and pop music. We were not allowed to sing that type of music. From the start of school, my teacher used me as a lead singer. This teacher worked with me, building my confidence to sing. I no longer was so sensitive, and I challenged some of my fears, which led me to participate in competitions for the school and pageants that opened the door for an offered scholarship.

When I left home for college, I left with a heavy heart leaving my family behind. My mom and brother escorted me to school. She stayed with me the entire day, ensuring I was well settled in and meeting the Dean and house mom. Feeling shy and a little lost, I quickly made friends with my room-mates, who were Christian as well but with different views about God.

We lived in an all girl's dorm. No men were allowed during a certain time of day and visiting girls' rooms was prohibited. Everything I ever learned from my mom was to always respect yourself and don't let anyone pull you away from God. She said, "I trust you to make the right decisions and remember I love you and always will support you."

I SURVIVED

Looking back over my life, I experienced the love of God on many diverse levels and each time, He proved himself that He loved me. I was always surrounded by prayer from my mom. God had His hands on my life. I was a young girl who lived in the deep part of the country called Shilo, with dirt roads and country stores that were 2 miles away. Everyone knew each other. They trusted their doors to be unlocked. They trusted people in the neighborhood around their children. But people from other cities and states would come and work on the farmland. Mostly citrus fruit during seasons.

My stepfather worked as a mechanic who had many visitors that came to him with car issues. As a child, I encountered some men making sexual comments or staring at me and I quickly gave them an evil eye of hatred. I wanted them to feel the anguish that I felt. When they came to our home, I would go inside the house until they left. I tried to always guard myself cautiously when my mother wasn't around.

My mom worked long hours 50 miles away with no phone. I stayed away from my stepfather to avoid his attacks with the punches he would inflict on me. I even wondered if I would reach 16 years old because he disliked me. But God gave me ways to stay out of his sight.

I soon found out years later that the man who attacked me had committed murder and was living a double life in our area. As I recount back on that day, I didn't realize I was in another city 15 miles from my home. I was not much of a runner, but at that time, God gave me the strength to get away from my attacker. I was trying to figure out a way to help myself as he drove until I heard God say, "Now." If I had stayed in the vehicle when he came to a complete stop, I genuinely believe I would not be alive today.

But God supernaturally lifted me out of that seat. I quickly opened the door to jump out and ran as fast as possible. I knew God had a plan for me. After traveling and praying with the pastor's wife, I experienced the power of prayer for the sick. I talk about wanting to know who God was. I found out that day when I was in trouble. He was there protecting me all along.

Dealing with the emotional scars that affected me, my mom was strong in faith and constantly kept my sibling and me in prayer. I never neglected my time with God. Those scars I carried inside me eventually caused me to have stomach ulcers. The medications the doctors gave me were too strong and it added more problems. As I released it from my mind, it became less painful. Through much prayer, I was healed not from medicine, but from the power of God. He dried those wounds up in my stomach.

I think about how God would show signs in the sky to me, mostly in clouds while they were moving. I would look to see His face or angels. I would have dreams which I didn't understand about people in the neighborhood. My mom would often tell us stories about God's goodness and mercy. She would gather all her kids around her to talk about how God healed her from the loss of her baby and pray God would keep her alive to rise us. We often watched my mom at the point of death in and out of the hospital so much that we feared losing her.

The saints from the church would come to our home and pray. God always turned the situation around. Healing would come to her body. Her doctors were amazed because they had told her she would not live long. But God had a plan for her. So, each time it rained, we stayed inside listening to my mom's stories and if it was bad weather, we were quiet because of the lightning and thunder.

Once it stopped raining, we would go back outside and find in our front yard beautiful silverfish, and they were always alive in the dirt. We didn't have any grass around our house and neither were there any lakes or ponds nearby, but there were many fish. We knew it was an act of God's doing but we didn't know why.

This happened many times until we moved, and another family moved in. We often wondered if they were experiencing the same thing, but we didn't hear anything. WE knew for sure after seeing the mysteries of God happen around that home, we were delivered and set free of the memories, especially for me because things changed for the better in every area of our lives.

Throughout my life, I encountered God's grace. But as much teaching as I was taught about life, I still made decisions that weren't always the best. There were times I just wanted to feel normal. I wanted more of God but in my own way. I had lived a sheltered life under the guardian of my mom. My college days caused me to mature quickly. I never went to school looking for love or marriage, but love found me. I thought I had found my soulmate. I was so in love that I compromised everything that I was taught about relationships and marriage. I thought to myself, "this man loves God and me."

Even though He believed in God, his faith was different than mine, which made us unequally yoked, as the Bible said. He wasn't saved but made many sacrifices to show his love for me. He showed me every reason to be his wife. I had married him and my life at that time was in a good place. Things were very good.

I had left church but soon started going back. He wasn't interested at all and many times, I was by myself in church. I never consider this part of my life without him. I wanted him with me to share the love of God. I prayed for him, but we couldn't agree about anything concerning church. I knew God had plans for me to serve Him one day in ministry, but I couldn't dream or see it happening with this man.

Too often, you find more wives and children in church without husbands, and I didn't want that for myself. I begin to seek God, inviting Him to take me back to the place we once shared. I was blind to love even when my ex would often praise himself for the achievements he accomplished without God's help. He would say, "God never helped me with anything. I did everything on my own."

I felt shattered by his words. My marriage soon after was unraveling slowly due to infidelity and children that came along with the affairs. Reality hit me hard. I was living in a fairytale world, thinking this couldn't be happening. I never felt so much pain going through a divorce. I was in a dark place, feeling depressed, betrayed, and embarrassed. I took my vow before God with honor, knowing that I would spend my whole life with this man.

I went into prayer hard for my marriage. I had become consumed with wanting God to fix it. After a separation, most people are left to fend for themselves, but I was blessed. God had him to continue to pay my bills for a lengthy period. I didn't see him much. I worked and stayed in church, which kept me busy. God was with me as I humbled myself before Him and He gave me peace in the midst of a storm.

I had to come to terms with asking God to forgive me and learned to forgive my ex. I realized I was held back by holding on to the past. But then God said, "Let it go and allow me to give you what I have." I received the strength of God once I surrendered all. The guilt, shame, and disappointment left me. Now, I wait on God for everything. God is faithful. He healed my broken heart. I learn to trust God and never compromise His word.

My life has changed. I see God's will for others come to pass. I began to obey Him as He trusted me with assignments to pray for many. For every assignment, He answered the prayers of every person He had assigned. I love missionary work. That will always be a part of my life. And still today, I welcome the work for ministry. I'm an intercessor that loves to pray because in my heart, I love to see people come out of bondage and experience the true love of God.

There is so much more to tell about my journey with God. I'm so grateful God gave me the opportunity to be part of Prophetess Kimberly Moses Ministries, which caused me to reach deeper into the presence of God.

<u>LESSON</u>

1. The love God has for me never changed, even when I was at my lowest and made decisions that didn't please Him.

2. I learned never to accept the norms and values of this world just because everyone else is okay with it and leave out the righteousness of God concerning His principles of right living.

3. I learned things of the world only offer you a quick solution that the enemy disguises to trap you.

4. I learned to ask God to teach me how to love those who wanted to stop my destiny.

5. I learned that this race isn't given to the swift but to the one who endures to the end.

6. I learned because of God's grace, I'm loved.

7. I learned to stand firm on the Word of God no matter how it looks. Trust and believe God's Word.

CHAPTER 12

The Wrong One

Letitia Sturkey

All our lives, we grow up hearing the word "NO." For example, "Can I have some cookies?" "No!" "Can you brush your teeth?" "No." No can be a frightening or rebellious word. Sometimes it can be a safety word or a word of encouragement. For me, the word "No" was suspicion, uncertainty, and loneliness.

At the age of 15, God called my name and I received Christ, the invisible guy that people spoke about in mysteries. The one everyone believed in. They were so convinced that I, too, believed in Him. I didn't know what I was doing or if even this new life I found in Jesus came with an instruction manual. I just knew I was different. I had my first Christian boyfriend, whom I adored. He was everything a girl could want: very sweet, cute, and funny. He kept me crying for a good reason, and that's because he was so hilarious that I laughed until I cried. I saw God's calling on his life and knew that I wasn't ready to make that commitment to submit to God fully. So when the opportunity arose, I let him go. About a few months later, someone I only knew as a friend began expressing that they had an interest in me in various ways. My boyfriend and I at the time had broken up.

"Well, you're a mama's boy, so maybe you should date her!" I said angrily. Trying not to choke on my tears, I felt so infuriated, especially because he always chose his mom over me. I could never understand their relationship, and they were so close. I guess because I never experienced anything close like that on my end. So getting rid of the problem was easier than dealing with it. (I saw this all my life when my mom raised us, it was easier to quit than fight). I wept and cried for days and even wrote a poem about my breakup titled "A Romance Lost In The Wind." I felt heavy and sad knowing that my buddy, my joy in the world was gone, but I knew it was for the best. People say, "If you love something, let it go and if they come back, then you will know." Well, I guess it wasn't love because someone caught my eye. Finally, after all the time he put into flirting, he let me know he was interested: my friend's brother. I started showing interest back by punching him. Yes, I was a little strange back then. I liked that he always seemed to take an interest in me, my day, in whom I inspired to be, and in who I was. We would sit and talk for hours, waiting for each other to hang up and create little rap verses for one another. I paid him no mind at one point, but eventually, I let my guard down. He heard that my boyfriend and me had broken up, so he jumped on the opportunity like white paint on a black easel board.

"So when are you going to be my girlfriend?" He asked. My heart began racing. I was so nervous that I replied, "Shut up," in the myspace messenger app. SMACK, the myspace sound effect played back. "Oh, you have jokes?" I said out loud as the sound of my acrylic nails echoed through the small studio apartment I stayed in. My smile was so wide. You could have mistaken my lips for boomerangs. Talk about butterflies. They were all around me. He gave me attention and thought I was cute. I didn't even have to try with him. This made me feel so special. I didn't know my dad at the time and maybe deep down, somewhere in the inside of me, I was looking for him in all the wrong places. As time went on, I began seeing all the "red flags." I remember going on a trip with my church called "youth explosion." It was a trip that brought multiple churches together to fellowship and worship in a place that wasn't the hood.

The youth bonded over this trip. This place is where I first got saved. As we all settled into our rooms, the youth, I began to prepare myself for the pool. I was looking for AJ: my boo and my baby. Come to find out, he was off with another girl on a boat. My heart was broken and I was so angry at both of them. I could just choke her and stomp him out. Before I could let my rage boil over, my ex came and comforted me. All honestly, he was the one that told me where he was. He also told me that AJ told him that he was just trying to get sex from me and that he cared nothing about me. I wasn't too sure about this because AJ never made a move on me and I felt my ex was just being sneaky. At that point, we just decided to hang out together. AJ and his godbrother walked in on us together, and like the alpha male he was, he decided to make a move. I made snooty little comments to him and decided to hop in the hot tub at that point. My ex saw how down I was and decided to follow. Then moments later, AJ came in too. Now the moment I wanted alone was filled with different people in my space. My ex grabbed one of my hands and was saying that he still cared for me and apologized for our break up. He also let me know that he would always be my friend and that what he told me was the truth. Next AJ came and grabbed my other hand and tried to pull me away from my ex. Then the next thing you know, I was the knot in the rope. I was being pulled back and forth like a tug of war. This is a memory I hold dear to this day because it's the only time he actually fought for me.

God warned me 3 times about AJ. Through various church leaders and prophets, He told me that he wasn't the one. I was 15 years old and literally just got saved. How was I supposed to know what to truly do with that information? My boyfriend's mother didn't really like me, so I felt she somehow persuaded the church members into trying to get me to leave him alone, especially because 98% of them were his family. Everything they prophesied went in one ear and out the other because I was so in love and blinded by the enemy that I chose to ignore these warnings.

I SURVIVED

My then-boyfriend, now my former husband and I had our first kid together. I gave him a baby girl. As the years went past, we had some more. We had three kids here on earth (and some aborted ones in heaven. I regret this until this day. We would have had a total of 11 kids.) We have two girls, one boy and one baby boy in heaven that passed away at four months old. God told me one day that I walked away from him for 13 years. At the time, I had been with my husband for 13 years. This saddened me because I always thought I was there. God came after me with conviction, but He loves me and it was time for me to go back home. I began looking for churches. God's presence touched me in the church that I attend now, so I made this my church home in 2016. Since I already had two kids with my husband, I began rationalizing my sin. I felt that AJ would always be the one I chose, so I pushed for us to get married. He constantly denied it. So I packed my things and headed for the door. He caught me and decided that he would marry me. This was music to my ears. Even getting the marriage certificate submitted was such a hassle. I was so blinded by my selfish desires that I overlooked all the red flags. I just thought marriage was a piece of paper and if we didn't work out, we would just get divorced.

God knows best. I married him— the wrong person. Since then, I have suffered many spiritual and physical death in my life. God says, "Satan comes to kill, steal and destroy, but I come to give you life and life more abundantly." Since I married my former husband, there have been multiple occasions of adultery. My sister was one of them and had a baby by him that she later aborted, He gave me an STD, but God healed me. I no longer have any trace of it in my body, and God protects me from ever getting it again. My husband left the marriage two or three times because he had lustful demonic feelings for her, better known as soul ties. I forgave my sister, let her back into my home, and it happened again. I had so much hate for this man. I couldn't care if he dropped dead. He stopped helping with bills around the house. We eventually got evicted and had to move into a shelter. I was pregnant again and found out he cheated some more. The list goes on and on. We recently had a baby boy in May 2020, during the pandemic. He passed away in the hands of my husband. It was an accident, but it brought more death upon me, my family, and us. This was an unbearable pain and it hurt so much. I began withholding sex due to anger and non-trust. I always ran away when I got the chance to. I just wanted to be free and never look back. A part of me still feels this way but God's grace and mercy pursues me to stay.

<u>THE LESSON</u>

I learned that when God tells you not to do something, He means don't do it. He keeps no good thing away from those who love him, so if there's something He is telling us not to do, then trust God and believe that whatever it is, it's not good for you. When you choose to go against God's Word, no matter what, it will NOT work out, or it will be a lot of suffering. I also learned that I idolized a man that couldn't do anything for me. I trusted him way more than I trusted God. Maybe I loved him a little more too. The fact that I could physically see AJ and not see God made it easier to love AJ. Over the years, despite what I did to God and most of all myself, God began slowly restoring my marriage. The invisible force I couldn't see began putting things back together when the physical man wouldn't.

If I had trusted God and not taken matters into my own hands along the restoration process, my son Lavelle would still be alive today. I learn every single day why God said NO. This life of suffering is not what God wants for me because he wasn't supposed to be my husband. I am 16 years behind in the spirit. I learned that I wasn't the greatest mom because I allowed my pain and suffering to spill over into my children's lives. I also learned that I wasn't ready to be one as well. God still has some cleaning up to do with me. I had so much trash inside of me that it began affecting my heart physically and spiritually. I became severely ill because of the hate and resentment toward my husband, his family, and mistresses. The scriptures came to life through me (*Proverbs 4:23, 15:13*).

I learned true love by staying in the marriage *(Galatians 5:22-23)*. Although sometimes my husband doesn't love me, God does. I don't feel God's physical touch, but He does show up on time when I need Him. He has shown me how to be a better woman to myself, my kids, and my husband. He is teaching me how to love like I've never been hurt. Marriage is a covenant to God, a promise. I never knew that, but I know that now. God wanted me to show my husband the same grace he showed me during the 13 years I walked away from him.

The last thing I wanted to do was pray for someone that caused me so much pain and suffering, but because I loved God, I yelled and screamed at God but eventually did it. This life taught me how to fight spiritually and although it is so much easier to give up on everything, especially marriage, God just won't release me. I am learning to trust God through the process. I'm learning that I can't respond the same way because Satan is literally trying to kill me physically and spiritually. It's not even about my issues. It's about what's literally inside of me. I always thought that sin bought this lifestyle, but it didn't because I am redeemed in Christ. This lifestyle that God chose to turn around comes with warfare because of WHO I am in Christ and not What I am. I encourage women every chance I get. Everything that glitters is not gold. PLEASE WAIT ON GOD. Be blessed!!

CHAPTER 13

Witchcraft

By Kimberly Moses

Growing up, I was fascinated with magic, witches, scary movies, and anything mystical. My first encounter with a witch was in middle school. Her name was Dawn and she would tell everyone that she was a good witch. The entire school talked bad about her because she was considered weird but I have always been drawn to the underdogs. Therefore I was nice to Dawn and she spoke to me. However, I was hurt and devastated when I heard about the tragedy in Dawn's life. When I went to school one day, one of Dawn's neighbors in our class came up to me. "Kimberly, did you hear what happened to Dawn's parents?" "No," I replied. "Her dad killed her mother and then killed himself. Dawn came home and found their bodies. She will go to another school now and live with some distant family." I was shocked and felt so bad for Dawn.

I felt like all witches could be nice because of my experience with Dawn. Yet I knew that to be false because of how they were portrayed on film and my experiences with them as a prophet. Several years went back and thoughts of witches weren't on my mind. I married, divorced, and was called into ministry. When God called me to preach His word, He revealed my purpose and told me that I was a prophet. At first, I had no idea what a prophet was. I rejected it because I said, "God, I am not an obese Caucasian man with a beard." However, the Lord showed me women prophets through Scripture. Once I started walking in the prophetic, the attacks of witchcraft came and I realized that witches were enemies of the Cross. I was stalked, harassed, violated, and attacked in various areas.

I SURVIVED

I was so excited once I found my purpose and researched everything possible about being a prophet. God put an anointing on my life to cast out devils and heal the sick. God was glorified, but the enemy was upset. I started teaching others about the prophets in the Bible and witches on social media began to take notice. A lady who had a form of godliness but denied the power thereof began to send my husband and I hate mail. First, she sent emails to every email account we had. Then she started sending mail to my PO BOX. The letters were sent regularly, so I told the postal clerk that I was being harassed and if a letter had no return address, do not put it in my box. The postal clerk and her supervisor got involved and reported to their chain of command the harassment. The letters were full of curses and how much she disliked and disagreed with what we were doing. We never read these letters but skimmed over them. We didn't want to get those negative words into our spirit because we knew the devil was using this lady who confessed to being a Christian to discourage our assignment. Then this lady mailed me a death certificate. It was around Christmas and there was a card with no return address in my PO BOX. I opened the envelope and saw the card. Inside of it was a death certificate that said, "I suffer not a witch to live." I immediately threw the card away in a dumpster. I thought it was ironic that this lady called me a witch when she was the one doing witchcraft, stalking, and harassing my husband and me. She was trying to curse me and all I do is bless people. She was very deceived and perverted. I had enough and went into serious warfare. I went to my apostle and he prayed. Finally, the attack was broken and the witch disappeared.

Another attack came when my pastor put me on a preaching schedule at church. God sent me to this church to serve after experiencing church hurt and not being a part of any ministry for a year. God elevated me there and I had my own keys to the church. I was amazed that I could go to church anytime I wanted and I was in leadership there in such a short time. However, this promotion came with attacks. One Sunday morning around 3 am, I was awakened by an evil presence that tried to attack me by holding me down. I rebuked it and it left, but then a horrible sickness came upon me. I felt extremely nauseous and had a headache. I prayed and asked God for strength to be able to preach in a couple of hours at 11 am. I tried to go back to sleep but felt too sick. I got up, praised, worshiped, and dressed, but the sickness was still upon me. I was thirsty and hungry, but I knew I would vomit if I ate anything and I didn't want to take the chance, especially since I had to stand in front of the church. I pressed my way to church and as the worship was going forth, I prayed for the Holy Spirit to help me. It was now my turn to preach and as soon as I opened my mouth to preach, the sickness went away as God's anointing to preach consumed me. The enemy tried to shut me down. After I finished preaching that morning, many people came up to me and praised God because the message was just for them.

Another time, I was lying on my couch and half awake. I felt evil enter my room but still laid on the couch with my eyes closed. Suddenly, I felt a hand enter my body, grab my soul, and pull. "Ouch!" I yelled out in pain. The hand let go and I felt my soul snap back into place. I knew it was my soul by supernatural revelation. I saw a light-skinned lady with long black bangs standing over me when I opened my eyes. I was horrified and when she realized that I could see her, she vanished. I jumped up in fear and anger. I felt so violated that this witch came into my home and tried to kill me. Our souls are immortal and live forever in eternity. The enemy tried to steal my soul but failed. Immediately I began to pray fervently, rebuking hell and the enemy. I was truly upset and when I calmed down, I heard the Holy Spirit whisper a name. I was led to go on Facebook and type in the name and I was shocked. The same lady who was just in my room earlier pulled up. I didn't understand how she found me because we weren't friends. I quickly realized how serious ministry is. The devil isn't playing around and I needed real power on my life for protection, so I made sure I drew closer to the Lord, fasted more, and prayed consistently.

A year later, I was doing a teaching on Facebook about a celebrity who sold their soul to the enemy. This teaching upset many people, and there was a witch present on the broadcast. I knew she was a witch supernaturally when I saw her profile photo. She shared my broadcast on her page and when I ended the video, I went to her profile. I noticed that she was following prophets, psychics, and witches. The next night this same lady astroprojected into my room around 2 am. I awoke to an evil presence and saw her standing at my bedroom door. She had a glass jar full of big beetles and when I saw her, I said, "Get out of here in the name of Jesus." Then she left but later on that day, I felt like something was choking me in the spirit. I couldn't see what was constricting around my neck in the natural, but when I entered prayer, it was revealed that snakes were attacking me and my eyes opened and I could see them trying to bite me. I couldn't believe I was experiencing a python attack. I asked some prayer warriors in my ministry to pray and when they did, I experienced temporary relief. However, this attack wasn't broken until my husband and I attended a conference and the presence of God descended upon me. I knew that I had to go higher. At this event, I discovered how to cut the silver cord *(Ecclesiastes 12:6-7)*. When we pray these prayers, if a witch has astroprojected, they will die because they will not be able to find their way back to their body. Since I received this insight, there has been no witches coming into my room.

A few months later, I was hosting my annual conference and a worker of witchcraft came to hurt me. However, this individual could not get close to me because I had discerning intercessors surrounding me and God's glory upon me. When I would stand up next to the wall during worship, this individual got out of their seat and tried to stand near me on the wall. One lady from my ministry stood between us and began to pray in tongues and this individual sat down in their seat. When it was my time to minister, the Holy Spirit told me to call out this individual and get some paper towels because they would be delivered. Well, I spoke what God put in my mouth and released his fire upon the individual and they fell out. When they came back to themselves, they purged up white foam. The enemy had a plan, but God thwarted it and got the glory.

Often, I have experienced great stabbing sensations all over my body. When these attacks first started, I walked through my home and said, "Lord what is that?" He said, "That's witchcraft." Now when I feel it, I know that someone is praying against me, so I immediately stop what I may be doing, rebuke it, pull out the dagger, and then throw them back to the witch. These attacks have kept me humble and deepened my dependency on God. I have become more aware of how much I love and need Him. He protects me from these attacks. One day I was driving and I felt a knife stab me in my thigh in the spirit. I yelled ouch and was getting ready to drive around a curve. Immediately my car began to stall out in the middle of the curvy road. I knew I was underneath a demonic attack. I prayed, laid my hands on my dashboard, and commanded the car to make it home. The car started back up and my children and I made it home. I was grateful that God protected us and didn't allow any cars to run into us while they were driving around the curve. God showed me the source of the attack and He handled it because the enemy can't curse what God has blessed. God is our defender and vindicator.

THE LESSON

1. Woe to Them That Call Evil Good And Good Evil *(Isaiah 5:20).*

The enemy has blinded the eyes of the children of darkness and their thought process is perverted. Sadly witches and others are enemies of the Cross because they are coming against God and His works in the earth. They hate God's servants and feel like they are right.

2. Sin Equals Death *(Romans 6:23)*

The enemy comes to kill, steal, and destroy. When we sin, we allow the enemy to come in and cause chaos and permit him to shorten our lives. The devil doesn't want us to be blessed or prosperous. He gives people stuff, but it's with strings attached. Some have sold their souls to the devil for fame or wealth, but they will spend eternity in hell.

3. The Flesh Profits No Good Thing *(John 6:63)*

The flesh produces no good thing. If you sow according to flesh, you will reap corruption *(Galatians 6:8)*. Witches try to curse people and cast spells but in the end they reap corruption. They don't realize they are only digging a pit from themselves. They might think they're powerful but their power is no match for the Lord Jesus Christ. Greater is He in us than Him that's in the world *(1 John 4:4)*.

CHAPTER 14

Witchcraft

By Jeanette Lewis

I graduated High School when I was 18 years old. I was young and unaware of my own identity. I did know what I wanted to do after graduation. I was uncertain of my wavering faith and irritated with the fact of going to church. I have been in church since my childhood because I had no choice in going. My family always went to church.

The times I didn't want to go to church, I dreaded it because Sunday was an all-day service event. Having Sunday school and church service combined is a common tradition in African American churches. My mother, a very stern, strong woman, was tough on her children. So on the bright side, going to church was my chance to be free. As an inspiring Christian girl, I wanted to remain faithful to my mother to gain her approval on the outside. But on the inside, I was betraying God by being a Christian for my mother and not for God.

My love for my mother is undeniable. She is a special part of my life. The night of my graduation plays like a movie frozen in time before me. I have unnoticed memories indistinguishable from reality. I can still hear the song in the auditorium. The melody swirls in the air as the principal announces the graduates.

As I lay still in my chair, enjoying my brief time of true freedom, I felt like sweet dew nectar. I was free from my mother's overbearing rules and the stressful high school years. I could not find peace at home or school.

As I lay still in my chair, enjoying my brief time of true freedom, I felt like sweet dew nectar. I was free from my mother's overbearing rules and the stressful high school years. I could not find peace at home or school.

I called upon God even though I was distant from Him. I needed His help to cope with a dysfunctional home and high school. I found peace only in the times when I called His name. I was seeking peace, but being 18, there was no escape from the horrific place I called home, not because of my mother but because of the witchcraft permeating its walls. My stepfather was a warlock. His sins were bearing on the household. There were times he would call my name to abed in his attempts at black magic. But at that time, I was only nine years old and naive, as all children are at a young age.

When my stepfather would call my name, I was hesitant but seeking not to anger my mother, so I listened to him. I would see the opened letters as my stepfather proceeded to hand me one. I was told to read the words. He told me that I would have good fortune if used correctly. My father could not read or write, so he needed my help reading the letters.

He had many powders: blue, purple, and black. The powders had no smell. It didn't make sense to me. The powder seemed nonexistent. The only reason I knew it was there was because I felt and saw it. They were so beautiful. I didn't realize at the time I was partaking in witchcraft.

My stepfather would proceed to put the powders on the doorways and instructed me not to bother it, but it was already too late. I had partaken in evil, so demonic spirits began to latch on to me and strange events began to manifest around me. I started having nightmares and while I was asleep, I would be forcibly awoken by a shadow yanking my hair hard, dragging me, and not attempting to release me until my hysterical screams could come forth. I would witness tall, dark beings walking through the wall in the darkness. My mother tried to console me, saying it was because I was misbehaving, but she didn't know what her husband was making me do; of the darkness he forced me to dance in.

My stepfather attempted multiple times to include my mother in his sin by playing with dark forces. Despite my mother's flaws, she was an unquestionably loyal Christian. She would not compromise with God by doing witchcraft or blending the two. That's why the safest place for me to sleep was with my mother. When night would come, the spirits would repeat the cycle of torture of grabbing my hair and surrounding me.

All these demonic attacks influenced my decision even more to leave home. So when the first chance presented itself, I took it. I moved in with my aunt and uncle. Shortly after, I got a job at a 5-star hotel as a maid service. I paid my uncle 50 dollars a week and saved my money. My uncle would begin to ask for extra money after I gave him the money for the week. He would try to take the extra money to buy more beer and cigarettes. My uncle did not work. He was a house husband. He would take care of the kids, cook, and clean.

My uncle was akin to a broken recorder replaying the same line. He would ask for money non-stop. To find peace, I would try to avoid him and take walks in the town. As I walked, I felt the cold air brush upon my skin.

As the moonlight bathed my skin, it glowed. I heard nothing but silence as the light poles aligned the street like stars.

Being in this peaceful environment led me to the place where the sound was explosive in the town by the loud music. On Friday, it was disco night. I was lured over there by the contrast of silence to sound. I was still at peace. I saw people drinking and dancing. Some were unable to move from excessive alcohol.

The environment that stood before me was different, but at the time, I had no idea that I was in the devil's domain. This night was the beginning of years of hardships because of one boy.

The environment sparked my curiosity because I was used to the church scene. In the Gospel, the dress code was appropriate clothing. It was a total difference from the club environment. I found myself smoking, drinking, and wearing provocative attire. I was in a daze. I knew I was out of place. In my mesmerized state, a boy approached me, telling me how fine and beautiful I was. I recognized him from school, but I didn't know him personally.

His smile portrayed surprise to see the church girl in a place like this. Being in this environment and hearing him tell me these things, I was happy. Then, abruptly he asked me, "Have you met my mother?" As he kept smiling, I was confused. "No," as I answered him, it dawned on my mind, "Why would he ask me that?" when I hardly knew him.

He found it very important for me to meet his mother. His mother lived a couple of houses down from us. Being ignorant of how weird this was, I would eventually agree to his request. As his persistence in me meeting his mother increased, we eventually left the disco. He took me to his mom's house. We went in through the back door that was facing the road. As we went into the house, I followed him to her room. She was on the floor with a friend. He yelled, "Mom," with enthusiasm and proceeded to tell her, "Mom, I would like you to meet my girlfriend," leaving me perplexed.

The room was filled with smoke from the marijuana in her mouth. It was an awful odor. My eyes were burning from the smoke. It was hard to breathe. I wanted to run out of the house to catch my breath. It was like holding your breath up under water for a long time, so you rush up for air. I maintained my composure until he was done speaking.

She was smoking around kids and that was weird to me. The red flags were there, but I was too naive to understand their kindness concealed their true intentions.

During this time, I rarely called upon God. I began to fall in love quickly with this boy. Quickly, we got to know each other intimately. God was aforethought. I felt that this boy was the one. My mother would try to visit often. She wanted me back home with her and her eyes conveyed pain that I wasn't with her so that she could protect me. She warned me that the boy was trouble and there were rumors about him all over town. She just wanted me to follow the ways of God, but I didn't listen and trouble would later find me.

I WAS TRIED

Time waits for no one. You find yourself living in that stream of time, never stopping, just following the current. I had two kids with the man I fell in love with at a young age. I was 24 years old on August 30, 1986. On Saturday, my children and I were invited to accompany their father's brother and sister to the prison where he resided at the time for charges of drug running. His brother was a previously convicted felon of manslaughter.

The environment I found myself in and the people I had as my associates completely contradict the way I was raised.

I knew this life did not suit me. At the time, I didn't know that I was being trapped in a fog of confusion, not seeing the truth like an addict saying he is not an addict and unknown to the dangers that lie before you. I knew that God never renounced me. I renounced Him. Love is dangerous. It can make you sacrifice what you know and believe in for others to be happy.

It was foolish to fall in love with someone who didn't share the same beliefs. As we were driving to the prison, the thoughts of feeling out of place and I don't belong here became intense. I felt awkward and confused about my thoughts about my religion or God. I felt like He was showing me I didn't belong with them, a warning that was not heeded.

I returned home and ignored the warning God showed me out of ignorance. Again, my brother-in-law arrived to take me to visit my children's father. This time I didn't feel awkward. God was silent like a day where the wind refused to howl. As we arrived, the kids got to see their father, and it was a good time.

We said our goodbyes and left. We started to head back. The silence God adorned was now falling off like a cookie crumbling to pieces. I began to see blackbirds in the sky. Feathers drowned in midnight, spots in the beauty of light as the sun shined down. They flew as graceful as the wind beside the driver's window. As they began to come even closer, the children became frightened. I embraced them, assuring them it would be okay. The birds started to land on the car, an omen unnoticed.

As quickly as it started, it ended as my brother-in-law stated he was pulling over. The birds left and he pulled over to a gas station. He bought everyone a barbeque sandwich. The aroma was strong. Our mouths were salivating at the thought of biting into them. As he started the car, he asked my son to sit next to him. I quickly shot down the idea. He loved my children with all his heart, but I didn't want him distracted as he was the driver.

He began to drive normally like he always does. I was sitting behind him, but the time began to slow for me. The Lord started to pursue my mind, which He catches easily and swiftly. His voice is unique, unexplainable, loud yet soft, stern but kind, fierce but soothing. He told me to move over from behind my brother-in-law and allow my daughter to sit there. The air becomes tense and the urge to pray goes through my body like an electrical current. I began to pray intensely and swiftly. No words were coming out but being understood by a greater force than myself, I called upon God for help. I did not know why I needed to, but everything told me to pray.

Then it's just quiet and suddenly an explosion of sound was in my left eardrum. Glass was floating in the air like a movie. I was breathless then the car flipped upside down in the air. Everything was moving slowly. Heads were moving side to side from the impact. I felt the same peace and absolute silence as when I was a child. It was the peace that I have always wanted.

At that moment, I learned what it means to attain true peace. It's when you're around death and there is no disorder but silence. BOOM! As the car hits the ground, it rolls over and over. When it stops, I know I'm alive. I feel immense pain in my left leg. I began screaming for my daughter and son. My voice was echoing in the silence. My eyes were closed because of the debris. I feel for my daughter as I'm holding my son. Her body is lifeless. My brother-in-law's arm is severed as he lays unmoving. My son only had a couple of scratches. My sister-in-law is okay. As I moved my daughter, her blood was everywhere. We get out of the car and I see the cause of the incident. An 18-wheeler semi-truck rammed into the small car head-on.

Paramedics would soon arrive due to me running down the road and getting the attention of three men. As I screamed frantically, the three men that had just come from fishing instructed me to place my daughter down as they rushed to give first aid. They told me about their fishing trip to calm me down. They told me they usually stay longer while fishing because there was always an abundance of fish out in the water, but today there were none to be seen as if they had disappeared.

The men were doctors. They began questioning me to see if I was okay, but all my concern was on my daughter. As they tried to resuscitate her, many thoughts overwhelmed me, "It was my fault. I was not good enough. I didn't protect her as a mother should. I failed."

As I was in a daze of thought, the truck driver began to apologize. He was just as shook as us. The paramedics arrived after the men called them during the attempt to save my daughter. We were escorted in the ambulance to the hospital. I was told that my brother-in-law had passed away.

The paramedics were driving at high speed. While in the back of the ambulance, they were also trying to save my daughter. My daughter was taken and placed in a helicopter as we arrived at the Ocala hospital. I was instructed to go to Shands hospital in Gainesville. It's a trauma hospital. My son finished getting stitches over his left eyebrow. My sister-in-law was heading home after receiving stitches on her forehead. Her mother and friend had picked her up.

My mother and brother rushed and picked me up after my checkup was done to rush to Shands hospital to be with my daughter. The accident took place at 4 in the afternoon and we arrived at Shands at 11:00 pm. 7 hours without me knowing if my daughter was alive or if she was leaving me to be with God.

I SURVIVED

I gave my name and my daughter's name to the receptionist, and the receptionist led me to go up the elevator to the trauma area. After I got off the elevator, I immediately went to find the nurse over my daughter. I was told that she had several injuries and had already received emergency treatment.

They had taken her into surgery shortly after she had arrived at the hospital. She had a pierced lung, severe brain damage, a broken left leg, and lacerations all over her face and body. The doctor then began to take us to her room and informed me that she was brain dead and that there was no brain activity. He said that the wounds could be treated but that since the brain was dead, there was nothing they could do and it was only a matter of time. She was on life support at the time. He extended his sympathy as he exited the room.

My mother was standing next to me as I received this information concerning my daughter. I thought that my world as I know it was over. This was my daughter. The child I was supposed to protect and love. A couple of hours ago, I held her, and she smiled at me. The times she was bad, I still loved her. When her brother was born, she thought that I had loved him more. In retaliation, she hit me in the head with a hard plastic toy leg while I was asleep. I was angry. She now had tubes in her mouth and needles in her body to keep her alive.

My mother didn't hesitate. With a booming bass in her voice, she grabbed her bottle of oil from her purse and began praying in her heavenly language. She was throwing oil on my daughter like she would when season-ing chicken. She was speaking that my daughter would wake up, she had to live, God has a purpose for her, God will get the glory, and He will emerge victoriously. The next couple of days were touch and go with my daughter's condition.

We stayed at the Ronald McDonald House for families with children in critical condition, so we didn't have to be far from her. My mother never gave up and knew that it was only a matter of time before she would wake up. God instilled in me a strange peace. I was not concerned because I knew He would work it out. One day in the hospital, I had to step out of my daughter's room to take care of my youngest son, who was cranky and needed me. My brother came to me where I was sitting and told me that my daughter was awake and was now talking. I rushed to my daughter's bedside with my son in my arms as I entered the room.

She said, "Mommy, I know uncle AL is dead." She was referring to my brother-in-law. I asked her how did show know that. She said, "I was with him and he told me that I couldn't follow him and that I would have to go the opposite way from the open the door and go back. As he walked towards the light, he turned around and said goodbye." That's when the doctor came inside the room and stood there like he had seen a ghost. The child that was supposed to not live but she survived. We were praising God for the miraculous miracle. The whole hospital was in an uproar. Everyone was calling her miracle child.

She had made the news in the Gainesville newspaper. The helicopter medical team also came to visit. Everyone had recognized that it was the work of God. But the work was not over yet. She had to wear a full-body cast and go to take many doctor's appointments and physical therapy to learn to walk again. The last doctor's appointments showed no brain injury or abnormalities.

She was later released from the hospital a couple of weeks later. Her recovery was quick and full of energy, like nothing had happened. She would later excel through elementary, middle school, and high school. She furthered her education to junior college and graduated with a minor in psychology. She went on to gain a bachelor's in science and her master's in nursing. The ordeal that we all survived drew me closer to God. I later found out that if I had been in the spot I put my daughter in, I would have died because she avoided most of the damage in the car because of her being small.

God knew what would happen. He wanted to draw me closer to Him and He had my attention. Ever since then, I never missed a moment without giving Him praise and I am now still the devoted woman of God. All of this was only the tip of the iceberg of what I would go through. Later on, God would be my only companion to never leave me in my darkest times.

My husband's mother would use witchcraft against my son and me. She blamed me for her son's death, who died at the age of 30. She cursed her own grandson and me. Later my son would die at the age of 30 and more would happen in my life. I didn't know at the time after the accident that there would be more trials and tribulations that stretched for years on.

My son has passed away. My husband has died and his mother is now dead. I'm surviving all the death and tragedies, that has been left behind by the battle of curses and witchcraft that was used. I thank God for allowing me to tell part of my story.

<u>**THE LESSON**</u>

I learned that the spirit world is real. When my stepfather asked me to read those letters, a demonic portal opened up in my life. I started getting attacked by nightmare spirits and married a warlock just like my stepfather.

I had access to the spiritual world at an early age. I was able to see things before they would manifest. I gave my life to God. He used what I knew of evil and turned it around for His good. My spiritual senses are very discerning. Sometimes I don't want to step into the spiritual realm because I feel I'm operating in self instead of God. The Lord reminded me I'm operating in him. There was a plot from the enemy to steal, destroy, and kill me from the beginning. But God had His hand guide me throughout this journey. I gave birth to children who would grow up to turn against me as if I were their enemies. I know the whole truth of that. If my stepfather or my estranged husband couldn't bring me down, the children I birthed would be the ones to finish the plan to destroy me. But God has already exposed them to me. I love the people who plotted to take my life. When God is for you, nothing in this world can touch you. I'm a living witness.

About The Author

Kimberly Moses started off her ministry as Kimberly Hargraves. She is highly sought after as a prophetic voice, intercessor and prolific author. There is no doubt that she has a global mandate on her life to serve the nations of the world by spreading the Gospel of Jesus Christ. She has a quickly expanding worldwide healing and deliverance ministry. Kimberly Moses wears many hats to fulfill the call God has placed on her life as an entrepreneur over several businesses including her own personal brand Rejoice Essentials which promotes the Gospel of Jesus Christ.

She also serves as a life coach and mentor to many women. She is also the loving mother of two wonderful children. She is married to Tron. Kimberly has dedicated her life to the work of ministry and to serve others under the call God has placed over her life. Kimberly currently resides in South Carolina.

She is a very anointed woman of God who signs, miracles and wonders follow. The miraculous and incessant testimonies attributed to her ministry are incalculable, with many reporting physical and mental healing, financial breakthroughs, debt cancellations and other favorable outcomes. She is known across the globe as a servant who truly labors on behalf of God's people through intercession.

She is the author of The Following:

"Overcoming Difficult Life Experiences with Scriptures and Prayers"
"Overcoming Emotions with Prayers"
"Daily Prayers That Bring Changes"
"In Right Standing,"
"Obedience Is Key,"
"Prayers That Break The Yoke Of The Enemy: A Book Of Declarations,"
"Prayers That Demolish Demonic Strongholds: A Book Of Declarations,"
"Work Smarter. Not Harder. A Book Of Declarations For The Workforce,"
"Set The Captives Free: A Book Of Deliverance."
"Pray More Challenge"
"Walk By Faith: A Daily Devotional"
"Empowering The New Me: Fifty Tips To Becoming A Godly Woman"
"School of the Prophets: A Curriculum For Success"
"8 Keys To Accessing The Supernatural"
"Conquering The Mind: A Daily Devotional"
"Enhancing The Prophetic In You"
"The ABCs of The Prophetic: Prophetic Characteristics"
"Wisdom Is The Principal Thing: A Daily Devotional"
"It Cost Me Everything"
"The Making Of A Prophet: Women Walking in Prophetic Destiny"
"The Art of Meditation: A Daily Devotional"
"Warfare Strategies: Biblical Weapons"
"Becoming A Better You"
"I Almost Died"
"The Pastor's Secret: The D.L. Series"
"June Bug The Busy Bee: The Gamer"

"June Bug The Busy Bee: The Bully"

"The Weary Prophet: Providing Practical Steps For Restoration"

"The Insignificant Woman"

"The Foolish Woman: A Daily Devotional"

"June Bug The Busy Bee: Sibling Rivalry"

"All Things Relationships"

"30 Day Pray For Your Spouse Challenge"

"The Christian Drama Queen Mentality"

"30 Days Praying For The Nations"

"Intercessor's Prayer Notebook"

"Prayer Request Notebook Fervent Effectual Prayers Of The Righteous"

"The Prophet's Notebook"

"The Photographer's Assistant"

"The Ultimate Entrepreneur"

"Diabetic Caretaker Blood Sugar Log"

"The Preacher's Handbook"

"Christian Weight Loss Journal"

"Couple's Recipe Meal Planner And Notebook"

"Prophetic Dreams And Visions Journal"

"The Therapist Secret: The D.L. Series"

"Tabuletta"

You can find more about Kimberly at
www.kimberlyhargraves.com

For Rejoice Essential Magazine, visit
www.rejoiceessential.com

For beauty, hair, and t-shirts, visit
www.rejoicingbeauty.com

Please write a review for my books on Amazon.com

Support this ministry:
Cashapp: $ProphetKimberlyMoses
Paypal.me/remag
Venmo: Kimberly-Moses-19

Follow my YouTube Channels:
Kimberly Moses
Kimberly Finds

Naseska C. Young is a native of Raeford, N.C. She currently resides in Fayetteville, N.C. She received her ministerial calling and was ordained as a minister in 2007. She has served as an usher, Sunday school teacher, armor-bearer, and praise and worship team leader. She is an inspirational writer, prophetic teacher of the Gospel, and gifted by the Holy Spirit in faith, speaking in unknown tongues, healing, intercession, and deliverance.

Her passion for writing began at an early age, but it wasn't until 2010 that she stepped out on faith at the age of thirty and published her first book entitled, *"Claiming Royalty: Understanding Who I Am As A Woman of God."* Following in 2011 was a novel entitled *"He Watches Me,"* and the sequel was published in 2012 entitled *"Nothing Can Separate Us."* In 2017, *"The Uncompromised Damsel: Purposeful Single Living Before The Vows"* was published. She loves to encourage and inspire people to become their best and discover their God-ordained purpose.

In 2016, she discovered the ministry of Prophetess Kimberly Moses and became a subscriber to her YouTube channel. In 2020, she wrote and contributed her first magazine article in *Rejoice Essential Magazine* entitled, *"Sexual Purity: Is It More Common Than We Think?"* Other articles she has written for the magazine include, *"Understanding the Seasons of Life with God," "Unleashing Your Spiritual Gifting,"* and "He Leads Me." She is currently an editor of Rejoice Essential Magazine.

Academically, she has acquired many certifications and a degree. She is certified as a Pre-School teacher. She has over twenty years in the medical field as a Certified Nurse Assistant with experience in several healthcare settings. She is a Registered Pharmacy Technician and a Medication Technician. She graduated in 2004 from Sandhills Community College with an associate degree in General Education. She is passionate about caring for others and will go the extra mile to provide the best care to those in her hands. She is currently working on completing a bachelor's degree in Health Science and she is pursuing her diploma in nursing as a licensed practical nurse. Education and achieving her goals are very important to her. She lives by the motto, "Sometimes You Have To Be Your Own Cheerleader." In life, there may be times when no one understands your goals and pursuit of success, but it is up to you to never let go of them because they are achievable.

In her spare time, she loves to spend time with family and friends, travel, and dine at nice restaurants. She is the oldest of five siblings. She strives to be a good example that her younger siblings can look up to for inspiration and support. Her favorite places to travel are to the beach and mountains to enjoy the beauty of nature, God's creation. Her favorite beach is Myrtle Beach in South Carolina and her favorite mountains are the Appalachian Mountains in Pigeon Forge, Tennessee. She loves Italian food. Her favorite restaurants are Olive Garden and Ruby Tuesday.

Sandi S. Pizarro is an upcoming inspiring event hostess. She is the owner of a production company and a small jewelry business. Sandi has been in ministry, AKA walking with Jesus, since 2000. She also uses her spiritual influence to encourage hurting women or women who just need an extra spiritual push in the right direction. Sandi and her husband of twenty years, Samuel, are the proud parents of three amazing children and the grandparents of two awesomely active grandchildren.

Brittany S. Myers is an author, motivational speaker, youth advocate, and creator of Daughters of Sarah Sanctuary. She is currently attending Beulah Heights University, majoring in Leadership Studies.

Before Brittany tapped into who she is in God, she had a troubled childhood and challenging young adulthood. At the age of 13, Brittany was placed in foster care. She has been in over 12 different group homes, foster homes, treatment facilities, short-term youth detention centers, and long-term detention centers. When she turned 15, she was committed to the Georgia Department of Juvenile Justice system and remained on probation until she was 21 years old. Those years of living amongst strangers were the hardest for her. Many would assume that she wouldn't make it out alive, free, or sane. She always kept her faith throughout her time, maneuvering through the child welfare and juvenile justice system. Her faith in God brought her through with a sound mind, resiliency, grit, and humility.

For several years, Brittany has advocated for the youth in the foster care and juvenile justice systems. She has championed alongside many child welfare agencies such as the Annie E. Casey Foundation, Georgia EmpowerMEnt, Multi-Agency Alliance for Children, Georgia Juvenile Justice State Advisory Group, and many other organizations. In 2017, the Georgia Association of Home and Services for Children and the Multi-Agency Alliance for Children publicly acknowledged and awarded Brittany for her tenacity to stand up for disadvantaged youth. She has done film work with Juvenile Film, exposing the complexities of the Juvenile Justice system. Also, she has spoken at countless events centered on educating youth in foster care about their rights and empowering them to overcome the obstacles they're facing.

In 2020, Brittany was inspired to write a book about the fruit of the Holy Spirit. During that time of her life, she was abandoned while pregnant. She told God that she wanted to stop filling her voids with men and truly heal and become the woman He had called her to be. In her time of consecration, God led her to study *Galatians 5:22-23*. She wrote a book titled *"The Fruit of the Spirt: 10-Day Devotional"* from that text. The Fruit of the Spirit: 10-Day Devotional encourages Christian women to develop a closer relationship with God and learn more about the nine attributes that indicate that a person is thriving in accord with the Holy Spirit.

Brittany is on a mission to empower women and disadvantaged youth. Her story of overcoming foster care, the juvenile justice system, and single parent syndrome pushes her to give back to her community by uplifting these vulnerable populations by utilizing strategic methods based on her expertise. She has an 8-year extensive background in leadership, public speaking, strategic sharing, consensus organizing, youth advocacy, youth support, mentoring, panel moderating, and team building.

Brittany lives with her family in Atlanta, Georgia. When she's not using her gifts to motivate others, she enjoys spending time with her children, shopping, and developing new skills.

If you like to get in touch with Brittany:

Email: **endlessblessings4us@gmail.com**
Facebook: **www.facebook.com/BrittanyVsCherry**
Instagram: **speakintothemicb**
Website: **brittanysmyers.com**

Jeanette Arlene Lewis was born on November 22, 1960, to Dorothy Jean Oglesby and Clifton Morley. Both of her parents are now deceased. Jeanette has one sister and five brothers. She also has five sisters and three brothers on her father's side.

Jeanette Arlene Lewis has been in church since her youth. She would later meet her father at the age of 11. Jeanette authored a book called, "Heavenly Treasures Within The Spirit, Body, Mind, and Soul," published in 2012. Jeanette has other books in the works that have not been published. She loves to sew, cook, decorate, garden, and read. She has a love for the beach and ocean. She loves to journal her thoughts and any important moments. Jeanette has always loved shoes, diamonds, playing pool, and bowling. She also loves music because it helps calm her mind and spirit during stress. Jeanette loves to play the bass guitar. God has blessed her regardless of what she might be going through. He instilled a love in her that she has for others. She thanks Him for that. Jeanette found herself in love with nature, the birds that fly in the sky, the monkeys that populate the forest and the song wind sings during early dew as dawn approaches. But her favorite thing that she loves is God.

Jeanette Arlene Lewis has three kids: one daughter and two sons. One son died during birth. My daughter is currently 39 years old and has a master's in nursing and a minor in psychology. She is the mother of three kids, twins and a boy.

Jeanette Arlene Lewis studied up under Pastor John D'Alesio at Heartland Christian Center. He was the first prophet to train her in the prophetic. He was a true mentor. The man of God taught Jeanette about speaking in tongues.

Jeanette Arlene Lewis attended the school of the prophets taught by the late Dr. Shelia J. Spencer. Her ministry was a time of refreshing in Jeanette's 6-months of training. She received a diploma. In honor of traveling the path of God, Jeanette was placed on a team with prophets which enhanced her connection to God even more.

Jeanette Arlene Lewis completed her third ministry training with Dr. Shawn Emanuel Carter and Pastor George Carter. Jeanette served as an armorbearer for Dr. Shawn Emanuel Carter as he traveled the world to different cities and states.

The path God placed Jeanette on would eventually lead me to Prophetess Kimberly Moses. Jeanette would be led to her by her sister, mentioning who she was. Jeanette would later join her mentor class, school of the prophet's class and then her advanced school of the prophet's class. It was refreshing. Jeanette was able to learn so much more than what she currently knew. She is watching prayers be answered and prophecies come to pass. She thanks God for this honor and opportunity to see this journey through and learn more.

Annette Darlene Stadmire was born in New Smyrna Beach, Florida, and raised in Oak Hill, Florida. She attended Bethune-Cookman University studying Elementary Education and minoring in Exception Education. Also, she attended Wolfson college in Miami, Florida, and studied Bonds Surety. Annette attended Florida Technical College in Deland, Florida, and studied Medical Coding and Insurance Specialty.

Annette has worked with The State of Florida Family and Children Services, where she reported and documented wellness checks on clients. She was employed with DOVE Villa Group Home as an Activity Coordinator. Later, she was employed with the Children Home Society as a foster parent and worked with Volusia County Schools.

Annette Darlene Stadmire was a member of Bible Way Church of God in Christ in Oak Hill, Florida. She joined Pastor Jerome Noble Ministries alongside Mother Ruth and under his direction of intercessory prayer in Miami, Florida. When she returned to North Florida, she set up under Pastor John Delesio Ministries in Orlando, Florida, and Nick Pena Ministries as a prayer intercessor in Daytona Beach, Florida.

Annette attended the Late Shelia J. Spencer Ministries and the School of the Prophets in Orlando, Florida. Annette has studied classes with Apostle Doctor Christian Harfouch Ministries in Tallahassee, Florida. Annette is presently under the guidance and direction of Kimberly Moses Ministries and her School of the Prophets.

In 2021, Annette started a pen pal ministry with women in prison. This ministry was birth through the leadership of Kimberly Moses Ministries. The women are encouraged to know their self-worth in Christ Jesus. Annette empowers them with the Word of God so that healing, deliverance, and salvation can take place in their wounded hearts to allow God's love to fill the void they long to want. Annette is so grateful for the presence of God in their lives. She is enjoying the journey with them.

Annette Darlene Stadmire loves working as a missionary, serving the needs of people. Her family was involved with feeding the homeless in the Volusia County area for years by handing out brown bag meals to different organizations and those on the streets. She enjoys watching nature shows, survival stories, miracle stories, westerns, and B/W movies classics. She loves gospel music but has a greater love for gospel instrumental smooth jazz music. When the weather is nice, she enjoys taking nature walks, driving in the country, and going to sporting events. Annette is a fan of stage plays. She loves writing because it relaxes her to think. She loves going to church and cooking for her family when they are together. This sums up a small portion of her life living for God and walking in her purpose. She loves her personal relationship with God. Her pursuit of God has given her a deeper revelation of His Word.

Gigi LaVonda Love is a mother of five adult children, two teenagers and the grandma of ten grandchildren. She and her two teenagers reside in Jacksonville, Florida. Gigi was called to ministry as an evangelist at twenty years old while living in Langenselbold, Germany. She began pursuing mentorship and learning how to fast, pray, study God's word, and learn how to be a young new wife and mother. After living in Germany for six years, Gigi LaVonda Love relocated back to her hometown of Glennville, Georgia, and later moved to Leesville, Louisiana, where she lived for almost twenty-three years. While in Louisiana, she fulfilled her dream of becoming a nurse and attended Louisiana Technical College, Lamar Salter Campus. Gigi LaVonda Love graduated in September 1999 as a Diploma Nurse and passed her nursing boards, gaining the title of Licensed Practical Nurse. Gigi later attended Northwestern State University, where she graduated, receiving her Associate's Degree in General Studies and after moving to Jacksonville, Florida, she completed her studies, graduated, passed her nursing boards and gained a higher nursing title as a Registered Nurse. Gigi never gave up on ministry as it was her God-given purpose to minister God's Word through preaching, teaching, and through song. Gigi is an anointed praise and worship leader that sings and prophesy through song as the Spirit leads.

While in Germany, Gigi was called to be an evangelist who believed God was working through her and could save everybody, and she still does. Gigi began to operate in the gift of healing, word of wisdom, word of knowledge, and prophesy. She continued to be studious in studying God's Word and living a fasted and prayerful lifestyle.

Gigi has had several supernatural encounters with God through Holy Spirit and is also a dreamer. God has even told Gigi what her name is in the spirit as she has gone through many tests and trials. Gigi loves to minister to all age categories and has a special love for single mothers. God told Gigi that her mission is to give everyone what He gave her, His love. There is no coincidence that her last name is Love. God confirmed that it is prophetic and in line with her kingdom purpose.

Gigi has been anointed as an intercessor and has a heart of compassion for the widow, orphan, poor and homeless. Gigi desires to make a difference through the leading of the Holy Spirit to see the fulfillment of the prophetic over her life to make a difference in Jacksonville, Florida, before moving on to her next assignment.

Gigi has been on the noon prayer call hosted by Prophetess Kimberly Moses ministry. She has had an article she wrote future in her March 2021 publication of *Rejoice Essential Magazine* and was featured on the cover of *Rejoice Essential Magazine November 2021*. Gigi wrote her first book collaboration with Dr. Zolisha Ware, entitled *Encountering Love* and her second book collaboration with Prophetess Kimberly Moses, entitled *All Things Relationship*, also in 2021. Gigi can be found on all social media platforms. She also laughed Gigi Love Ministries in January of last year. You can find her on:

Facebook**(LaVonda Gigi Love and Gigi Love Ministries)**
Twitter**(eldergigilove49),**
IG **(Gigi L Love),**
Clubhouse and Facebook Messenger,
Youtube**(Gigi Lov**e).
Her email is **gigiloveministries.com;**
P.O. Box 66175
Jacksonville, Florida 32208;
904-310-2839.

Letitia Sturkey formerly known as Letitia Flynn, was homeless almost all her life. Her mom was in and out of shelters, and then the pattern trickled down to her. Letitia began experiencing the supernatural at the age of 10 years old. Like any other child trying to find their place, she started drinking, hanging with the wrong crowd, and dressing provocatively. At the age of 13, God took it all away. She didn't even know who He was or if He truly existed. Letitia Sturkey wanted to know who the questionable figure was about two years later. She began seeking churches and eventually found a church home in Brooklyn, New York, off of Thomas. S. Boyland St. At the age of 15, she received salvation and allowed God to lead her life. God began walking with her. Mrs. Sturkey is the oldest of a sister and the second oldest of two brothers.

Coming from a home of filth, drugs, suicide, and molestation, she decided that she would die trying to live or fight her way through survival. She then ran away at the age of 15 and her new found journey began. Facing over 30 years of homelessness (in and out of the womb), God blessed her with her own apartment, a car, four beautiful children, including the child that was called to be with the Lord and a husband in whom she has been with for 16 years and married for 4. She is a loving wife, devoted mom, and a best friend to many. She loves to journal, write, sing, and write poetry in her leisure time. She loves feeding the less fortunate, volunteering her free time, and dancing. God blessed her with a dance ministry and she loves ministering when she can. She currently attends her new found church, "In the Light Ministries," in Lancaster, Pennsylvania, 17602. Since then, God has begun to open many doors and various people have asked Letitia Sturkey to participate on many platforms. She is a very strong believer in God and looks to erase the evil global footprint!

Keima S. Sinclair is a woman of faith, a Bible believer, and a servant of Heavenly Father God through the Lord Jesus Christ. She delights in prayer, praise, worship, dance, and ministering.

Keima is a mother, entrepreneur, and author. She is passionate about writing and speaking about the miracles of her life. She desires women and their children to learn to trust in God with all their problems and challenges they will face in their lives; for their salvation, deliverance, success, and blessings with their life fully dedicated to Father God and their walk in Christ Jesus. She desires families to be equipped with Heavenly tools (the Word of God and walking by faith, not by sight). These divine tools can be used accordingly for empowerment, to be victorious, overcomers, and more than conquerors for our God-given calling and purpose through Him who loves us unconditionally with an everlasting love.

Education
Nursing Assistant Certificate, Edison NJ Job Corps
Completed Human Resources Certificate Course, Cornell University, NY.
Certificates of Completion - Morris Cerullo GVA School of Ministry

Hobbies
Keima enjoys creating natural hair products, skin care, oral health care, ear health care, and benefits for the promotion of healing: pain relief and inflammation from the outside in, beautifying, anti-aging, and overall wellness). Many people have been blessed and helped with improvements concerning their conditions using her natural blends. Keima continues to work on her craft and plans to turn her hobby into a business.

Keima has traveled around the world for a business trip and has been to countries in Europe, such as Amsterdam and Ukraine. She experienced God making a way and making this all possible.

Other hobbies and interests are fishing, canoeing, sightseeing nature, horses, dolphins, turtles, and having goldfish as pets. She enjoys watching Christian Comedy and Faith-based movies, including films based on true events and true stories that are inspiring and edifying.

Film-TV

At 17, Keima was an extra in the film 'Private Parts.' She played the part of being a college student in a Community College in Bronx, New York, in the true story of Howard Stern.

In 2014, Keima appeared and participated in a demonstration on an episode of Doctor Oz at the ABC Studios in NYC, while Dr. Oz taught his audience and explained the benefits of Walnuts. Her younger sister accompanied her and was a part of the audience.

Ministry

Missionary domestic trips: co-ministering, praying and group singing for others in a Senior Citizen home in Paterson, New Jersey.

Ms. Sinclair enjoys street ministry, praying for people, and sharing Gospel tracks to help their relationship with God the Father through Jesus Christ. She is ecstatic about getting her children involved in making home-cooked meals during the holidays or other times for the homeless and serving them with personal items.

Volunteer Services

General Hospital in Passaic, New Jersey

Keima transported patients to the hospital in her early teenage years.
Faces of Fallen Fathers in the Great City of Paterson, NJ

Keima helped and served the community and has helped set up and organize the food and household items, and personal products to support the children and families who have lost their fathers due to violence and everyday people at her sister's organization.

Keima can be contacted via email or Facebook:
E: **keeplookinguptothehills@gmail.com**
FB: **https://facebook.com/lookinguptothehills**

ALLENA DOUGLAS BRATHWAITE is a humble servant of God. Allena is a speaker whose platform tells others about God's grace, mercy, and wondrous miracles. Allena's passion is working in different outreach ministries, sowing and providing essential items to the homeless, single mothers, teen mothers, sick and shut-in, and domestic violence victims. Allena is a woman who trusts God to bring her through real-life challenges — amazed by the wonder and faithfulness of God to do that and more. Her passion is to spread the Word to whom has an ear to hear. Allena is happy to report that she enjoys working with her husband in the ministry. Our ministry is JAB Deploying Love Ministries. It is a blessing bag ministry. We fund our ministry. Our ministry is geared to The Homeless Population and shelters. We always add a seed of five dollars to each backpack or bag.

5 is the number of grace. I have been asked many times, "Why do you give them money? They can buy drugs, alcohol, and cigarettes. I do this because God has shown me grace and mercy many times in my sin, foolishness, and life. I release the seed and it's up to people to do what they feel. Allena believes her ministry thrives from the overflow because of her relationship with God and that she is a cheerful giver. I believe one should empower themselves to:

•   That our challenges experience the presence and power of God in their everyday life. Trials are what build our Christian character by challenging our faith and teaching us to trust God fully.
- We are overcomers and are victorious through our walk with Christ.
- Look to Jesus, who is the hope and healer of all wounds.
- Believes there is triumph despite tragedy

Allena also knows what it is to hurt deeply. After losing her mother to an aneurysm and her grandmother gained her wings 12 hours later. She struggled with grief for 12 years. She isolated herself from her home state of LA for 12 years. Allena found ultimate peace and healing by trusting God and His promises.

Allena is a Registered Nurse who has practiced for greater than 30years. Allena is currently working with the Army Behavior Health population. Her hard work, advocacy, and passion are reflected in all she meets. There have been many trials working in this system. It is a politically driven, hard test and trials encountered, exposed to various personalities and religions. You must really be anchored in Christ and beliefs and have a strong prayer life. Allena is an advocate for domestic violence victims. She was formerly a charter member of The Liberty County Domestic Violence Task Force.

Allena is a Brain Aneurysm Survivor. Allena continually tells others of her miraculous recovery. Allena is a strong advocate for brain aneurysm awareness. She is supportive of others through many platforms and engages and lobbies legislators and congress to bring more awareness and funding for research. Allena and her husband Jose both work in the healthcare industry. They survived COVID 19 twice. Allena resides in Hinesville, GA, with her husband, Jose. Allena is the mother of 4 adult children, two bonus daughters, and 12 grandchildren.

Arlene Housey grew up in Clyo, Georgia, a small town in rural South Georgia. At an early age, she joined Mt. Pisgah Independent Methodist Church. Arlene Housey attended the public schools of Effingham County. She is a mother of two amazing daughters. She graduated from Armstrong Atlantic State University, now Georgia Southern University. She holds a master's degree from Cambridge College in Education. She is currently an educator with over 20 years of teaching experience. She was a basketball coach and tutor. She is very active in her local church and community, helping people love God. She has a desire for ministry to empower people through prayer. Arlene established a ministry called The Love and Healing Project. The ministry is based upon faith and the love for God. She has written articles in Rejoice Essential Magazine, published by Kimberly Moses.

Index

3

3rd grade, 16, 17

9

9-1-1, 68

A

abandonment, 5, 6
Abandonment, 3, 5, 6
abortions, 101
Abraham, 49
AC, 96
accident, 112, 128, 131
accidents, 3
achievements, 105
adored, 18, 108
adult, 5, 146, 153
advocate, 13, 84, 140, 153
affairs, 34, 41, 105

affirmations, 38, 39
afraid, 2, 12, 25, 31, 46, 49, 77, 82, 98, 100
African American, 18, 121
airplane, 25, 29
airport, 27, 28, 29, 63
AJ, 110, 111, 112
alcohol, 44, 124, 152
Allena, 57, 80, 152, 153
alpha, 64, 110
alumni, 63
ambassadors, 71
ambulance, 96, 97, 128
Amsterdam, 26, 27, 28, 150
Amusement Park, 28
Anemia, 69
Angela, 59, 61, 62, 82
Anger, 64
Annette, 93, 144, 145
anoint, 21
anointing, 82, 91, 116, 117
antioxidants, 71
anxiety, 5, 69
apartment, 6, 7, 8, 32, 46, 48, 69, 72, 86, 109, 148
apostle, 58, 117
argument, 8
Arlene, 11, 142, 143
armor-bearer, 137
armorbearer, 143
artery, 68
assignment, 3, 10, 49, 76, 106, 116, 147
assistant principal, 52

D

dark forces, 123

darkness, 2, 42, 120, 123

Darren, 60

dashboard, 119

daughter, 1, 8, 11, 13, 14, 17, 25, 29, 59, 81, 82, 99, 127, 128, 129, 130, 131, 142

daughters, 17, 101, 153

Daughters of Sarah Sanctuary, 140

David, 1

Dawn, 115

DCCS, 84

Dean, 62, 102

Dean Ruby Higgins, 62

death, 5, 11, 14, 57, 58, 61, 63, 64, 66, 67, 70, 83, 85, 90, 91, 92, 104, 111, 112, 116, 127, 131

debts, 40

Declarations, 134

dedication, 18

deep water, 72

defender, 120

deliverance, 16, 31, 91, 133, 137, 144, 149

Demolish, 134

depressed, 68, 105

depression, 54, 62, 66, 69

destroy, 10, 31, 111, 120, 132

detention center, 53, 55

Detroit, 26

devil, 8, 31, 38, 67, 70, 74, 79, 87, 91, 116, 118, 120, 124

devils, 116

diagnosis, 57, 68, 69, 73, 75, 98

diamonds, 142

E

H

hairs, 72

hands, 21, 27, 70, 102, 110, 112, 113, 119, 138

happiness, 11

harassed, 116

harassment, 116

hardship, 72

hasty, 30

hatred, 102

headache, 117

heal, 11, 63, 84, 85, 87, 116, 141

heart, 1, 4, 11, 17, 19, 22, 24, 30, 35, 41, 43, 47, 49, 50, 53, 61, 62, 64, 68, 69, 75, 81, 89, 100, 102, 106, 109, 110, 113, 127, 147

heart attack, 68, 69

heartache, 57

heaven, 3, 4, 14, 50, 85, 111

helicopter, 128, 130

hell, 3, 118, 120

hindrance, 59

Hinesville, 153

HIPPA, 84

holy, 51, 59, 100

Holy Spirit, 4, 21, 27, 36, 58, 59, 67, 72, 76, 79, 117, 118, 119, 137, 141, 146, 147

homeless, 145, 147, 148, 150, 152

Homelessness, 3

Honda Pilot, 45

honey, 14

honor, 2, 18, 35, 62, 63, 66, 105, 143

hope, 4, 23, 39, 43, 56, 64, 65, 91, 152

hospice, 14

January, 69, 83, 84, 147

jazz, 145

Jealousy, 6

Jeanette, 121, 142, 143

Jehovah, 9

Jesus, 2, 3, 4, 16, 26, 27, 35, 36, 42, 46, 55, 56, 64, 74, 75, 78, 90, 91, 93, 95, 98, 99, 100, 108, 118, 120, 133, 139, 144, 149, 150, 152

Joe, 60

jokes, 95, 109

Joseph, 1

Journal, 135

journey, 3, 12, 18, 21, 63, 64, 65, 106, 132, 143, 145, 148

joy, 4, 11, 29, 34, 93, 97, 109

judge, 55

July, 76

Juvenile, 3, 55, 140

Juvenile Film, 140

juvenile justice, 53, 55, 140, 141

juvenile justice system, 53, 55, 140, 141

K

Keima, 16, 23, 149, 150, 151

KFC, 48

kid, 53, 111

kill, 1, 2, 31, 82, 91, 98, 111, 113, 118, 120, 132

Kimberly Moses, 1, 44, 86, 106, 115, 133, 136, 137, 143, 144, 147

kingdom, 1, 66, 147

Kingdom, 30

knowledge, 34, 146

L

O

purpose, 3, 31, 37, 41, 42, 49, 92, 116, 130, 137, 145, 146, 147, 149
python attack, 118

Q

quarantine, 81, 82

R

racial divide, 67
radiation, 67
Raeford, 67, 72, 137
rage, 46, 110
rains, 1
rap verses, 109
raped, 1, 100
Real Estate Investors, 17
reap, 10, 40, 120
rebellious, 1, 108
receptionist, 129
recover, 11, 77
red blood cells, 69
red flags, 110, 111, 125
Red Lobster, 48
refrigerator, 20
refuge, 12, 57
Registered Pharmacy Technician, 137
Registered Respiratory Therapist, 45
registration, 48
rehabilitation, 58
rejected, 1, 61, 116

World Changers Church International, 54
worrying, 1
worship, 34, 49, 56, 74, 77, 79, 110, 117, 119, 137, 146, 149
writer, 137

CPSIA information can be obtained
at www.ICGtesting.com
Printed in the USA
BVHW030547230722
642834BV00006B/69